# CHANGING LIVES
## Lawyers Fighting for Children

❧ **LOURDES** ~~ADO, EDITOR~~ **ADO, EDITOR** ❧

"Changing Lives: Lawyers Fighti ~~dren~~ lren *puts children first and actively describes the valuable role highly* ~~trained and~~ *skilled lawyers can play in changing the odds for our most vulnerable children.*"

—**Marian Wright Edelman**
President, Children's Defense Fund

FIRST
CHAIR
·PRESS·

Cover design by Jill Tedhams/ABA Publishing.

Printed in the United States of America.

18 17 16 15 14 5 4 3 2 1

**Library of Congress Cataloging-in-Publication Data**

Rosado, Lourdes, editor.
  Changing lives : lawyers fighting for children : stories of attorneys making a difference in the lives of our most vulnerable children / by Lourdes Rosado, editor, First Chair Press.
    pages cm
  Includes index.
  ISBN 978-1-62722-508-3 (alk. paper)
1. Legal assistance to children--United States. 2. Children--Legal status, laws, etc.--United States. 3. Child welfare--United States. I. Title.
KF337.5.J88R67 2014
344.7303'27--dc23

2014008269

Discounts are available for books ordered in bulk. Special consideration is given to state bars, CLE programs, and other bar-related organizations. Inquire at Book Publishing, ABA Publishing, American Bar Association, 321 N. Clark Street, Chicago, Illinois 60654-7598.

www.ShopABA.org

# CONTENTS

# American Bar Association
## Section of Litigation
# CHILDREN'S RIGHTS
# LITIGATION COMMITTEE

The Children's Rights Litigation Committee (CRLC) was created by the Section of Litigation of the American Bar Association to address the vast underrepresentation of children in all aspects of the legal system. The CRLC's vision is to improve access to justice, engage pro bono lawyers, and improve outcomes for all children who come into contact with the legal system.

The CRLC's goal is to ensure that every child in need of legal assistance receives a well-trained lawyer, and thus the CRLC endeavors to increase the number of children's lawyers, legal projects, and pro bono attorneys representing children. The CRLC also develops training materials—such as the award-winning video *Interviewing the Child Client*—and creates and runs webinars and live education programs to assist advocates in providing the highest quality of representation for children. The CRLC develops model policies and standards on lawyering for children and provides technical assistance and training to individuals and groups who wish to start children's law programs. The CRLC works with children's law organizations around the country and maintains the online *Directory of Children's Law Programs*.

The CRLC achieves its ambitious agenda through the work of three cochairs, a nine-person working group of children's law and litigation experts, more than three hundred members, and a committee director. The CRLC's work is supported through the commitment and generosity of the Section of Litigation.

To learn more about the committee, visit the CRLC Web site, http://apps.americanbar.org/litigation/committees/childrights/, or contact the CRLC committee director at Cathy.Krebs@americanbar.org.

# ACKNOWLEDGMENTS

The editor and authors extend their gratitude to the following law interns for their invaluable research assistance: Jesse Dong, Tiara Greene, David J. Hanyok, Nishi Kumar, and Emily Poor.

We also express our great appreciation to the Section of Litigation of the American Bar Association for starting the Children's Rights Litigation Committee (CRLC) and being champions of CRLC's vision: to improve access to justice, engage pro bono lawyers, and improve outcomes for all children who come into contact with the legal system.

This book is dedicated to all the passionate and talented attorneys who already are devoted to this cause.

# AUTHOR BIOGRAPHIES

**Diane Baird** (B.S.Ed., Oklahoma University; M.S.W., Tulane University Graduate School of Social Work) is a licensed clinical social worker and an instructor in the Department of Pediatrics at the University of Colorado School of Medicine, at the Kempe Center for the Prevention and Treatment of Child Abuse and Neglect. She holds a bachelor's degree in education and earned her master of social work from Tulane University Graduate School of Social Work. Her clinical work involves parent-child interactional evaluations and treatment, infant mental health, child and family therapy, therapeutic visitation, and postadoptive intervention. She is particularly interested in rehabilitation of parent-child relationships following abuse or neglect. Ms. Baird's interest in attachment and early childhood development is central to her clinical work; she has served as an expert in this area for the State of Colorado Department of Human Services (DHS) for more than 15 years. Ms. Baird was a child welfare caseworker and supervisor before beginning her employment with the Kempe Center in 1986. Her position is currently in the Training, Education, and Consultation Program at the Kempe Center. There, Ms. Baird codirects the State and Regional Team (START), a multidisciplinary consultation group that has reviewed complex cases of child maltreatment, from a civil and/or criminal perspective, for more than 20 years; cases may be referred from Colorado, Nebraska, Montana, Wyoming, Alaska, and other states in the region. Ms. Baird writes curricula, provides training for Colorado DHS and the State Judicial Office, and collaborates with other states in the region to develop and offer training to child welfare staff.

**Gail Chang Bohr** (B.A., Wellesley College; M.S. in social work, Simmons College School of Social Work; J.D., William Mitchell College of Law) is a judge in the Second Judicial District of Minnesota. Before her election as the first Asian American judge in Ramsey County, Second Judicial District,

Judge Bohr was the first executive director of Children's Law Center of Minnesota (CLC), where she initiated programs to provide representation to children in the foster care system. In addition to representing children in court, managing and consulting with more than 270 CLC pro bono lawyers, and advocating for system reform, she has been co-counsel in 21 federal and state court appeals. Judge Bohr participated in the making of the American Bar Association (ABA) DVD *Interviewing the Child Client*, and taught trial advocacy for the National Institute of Trial Advocacy. She served as faculty for CLC's training programs for pro bono lawyers who represented children in the foster care system. She has written many articles on due process rights and the representation of children, and she has served on national and statewide committees, including the ABA Section of Litigation's Children's Rights Litigation Committee Working Group, the ABA Project for Judicial Excellence in Child Abuse and Neglect Proceedings, the Minnesota Juvenile Justice Advisory Committee, the Ramsey County Juvenile Court Children's Justice Initiative, and the Hennepin County Juvenile Court Children's Justice Initiative. Immediately after law school, Judge Bohr clerked for Minnesota Supreme Court Chief Justice A. M. "Sandy" Keith and practiced law at Faegre & Benson LLP. Judge Bohr has received awards for her work as a child advocate. In June 2008, she was named one of the top ten legal newsmakers of the decade by *Minnesota Lawyer*. In 2007, she received the American Bar Association's Child Advocacy Award, the William Mitchell College of Law Warren E. Burger Distinguished Service Award, and the *Minnesota Lawyer* Outstanding Service to the Profession Award. Before becoming an attorney, Judge Bohr had a 19-year career in clinical social work with children and families. Judge Bohr was born and raised in Kingston, Jamaica, of Chinese parents, and she is the ninth of 15 children.

**Jenny Chau** (B.A., University of California, Los Angeles; J.D., Whittier Law School) is an attorney who specializes in special education law. Ms. Chau began advocating for special education rights while in law school, in the Whittier Special Education Clinic. She continues to advocate for children with disabilities to obtain services and support through school districts, regional centers, and insurance companies. Ms. Chau is a member of the Educational Civil Rights Accountability Project of the Children's Rights

Litigation Committee of the American Bar Association's Section of Litigation; as part of that project, she is participating in work to promote the efforts of the federal Department of Education's Office for Civil Rights to monitor discrimination in schools.

**Franchesca L. Hamilton-Acker** (B.S., University of Louisiana at Lafayette; J.D., Southern University Law Center) is the managing attorney of the Child in Need of Care (CINC) Unit at Acadiana Legal Service Corporation in Lafayette, Louisiana, where she promotes an assertive and holistic approach to the representation of children in dependency proceedings to ensure that every client has a voice. Mrs. Hamilton-Acker oversees this representation in southwest and central Louisiana, a region encompassing more than 19 juvenile jurisdictions; the role includes overseeing the involvement of pro bono attorneys. Mrs. Hamilton-Acker joined the law firm of Acadiana Legal Service, in 1995 as a college intern. She decided to devote her career to public interest soon thereafter. Mrs. Hamilton-Acker returned to Acadiana Legal Services each summer while in law school as a law clerk. Upon graduation from law school, she returned to Acadiana Legal Services, where she worked in the Litigation Law Unit practicing housing, consumer, elder, and juvenile law. During this time, she represented clients in dependency, education, housing, and child welfare cases. In 2010, Acadiana Legal Service Corporation created the CINC Unit, which focuses primarily on representing children in dependency proceedings. Mrs. Hamilton-Acker has made a career choice of public-interest law, with a commitment to pursuing access to justice for all, especially the voiceless. Mrs. Hamilton-Acker is currently on the Louisiana Child in Need of Care Legislative Task Force, the Advisory Committee to the ABA Center on Children and the Law, and the working group of the Children's Rights Litigation Committee of the Section of Litigation in the American Bar Association.

**Rosa K. Hirji** (B.A., University of California, Santa Cruz; J.D., University of California Hastings College of the Law) is an attorney and owner of a firm that focuses on the educational, civil, and disability rights of youth, including court-involved youth. She represents youth and their families at all levels of administrative proceedings and in state and federal court. As a founding member of the Los Angeles Juvenile Court Education Panel, she is regularly appointed to represent young people in foster care, juvenile hall, and other institutionalized settings. Ms. Hirji is a former teacher with the Los Angeles Unified School District and a cofounder of the Dignity in Schools Campaign. Her practice has a public-interest orientation that strives to obtain relief that brings a wider impact for youth and communities. Ms. Hirji was appointed in 2012 as cochair of the Children's Rights Litigation Committee (CRLC) of the Section of Litigation, American Bar Association (ABA). She has been an active member of the ABA since 2003 and serves as the chair of the CRLC's Education Subcommittee. She is a member of the editorial board of *Children's Rights*, CRLC's quarterly newsletter. In 2004, she was awarded the Outstanding Subcommittee Chair Award by the ABA's Section of Litigation.

**Ira Lustbader** (B.S., State University of New York at Albany; J.D., Boston University School of Law) is an attorney and the associate director of Children's Rights (www.childrensrights.org), a national nonprofit children's advocacy organization based in New York City, which has led numerous efforts over the past 17 years to reform failing public child-welfare systems. Children's Rights, with active reform campaigns in more than a dozen states nationally, combines grassroots case-building and legal action infused with policy expertise to achieve court-ordered reforms, negotiated settlements, and, ultimately, improved outcomes for abused and neglected children. Since joining Children's Rights in 1999, Mr. Lustbader has been deeply involved in many of the organization's legal reform campaigns. He focuses on overarching strategy, development of national coalitions and partnerships, and organizational management. Before joining Children's Rights, Mr. Lustbader practiced law at Wolf Haldenstein Adler Freeman & Herz, LLP, in New York City, concentrating on national plaintiffs' class action litigation in consumer fraud, securities fraud, and antitrust cases. Before that, he handled matters on the defense side involving products liability and malpractice at the firms of Parker Chapin Flattau & Klimpl LLP and Bower & Gardner, both in New York City. From 1998 to 2006, Mr. Lustbader served as a board member of Neighborhood Youth & Family Services, a large nonprofit family preservation agency in the South Bronx. He is a past chair of the Committee on Public Service and Education at the Association of the Bar of the City of New York, and he is currently a member of the working group of the Children's Rights Litigation Committee of the Section of Litigation of the American Bar Association, the National Lawyers Guild, and the National Association of Counsel for Children.

**Candace Mitchell** (B.A., Columbia College) is currently a dual-degree student at New York University School of Law and Harvard Kennedy School. She is passionate about racial and economic justice and intends to work as a public defender upon graduation.

**Brent Pattison** (B.A., Wesleyan University; J.D., University of Minnesota) is an associate clinical professor of law and director of the Middleton Children's Rights Center at Drake University Law School. Mr. Pattison began his career as a Soros Justice Fellow at TeamChild, an award-winning program in Washington State that provides civil legal advocacy for children in the juvenile justice system. He has represented children in a wide variety of contexts, including delinquency, child welfare, housing, public benefits, and education cases. He is also a former special education teacher. Mr. Pattison currently teaches the Children's Rights Clinic at Drake University Law School, supervising law students who represent children in abuse, neglect, and delinquency proceedings. He also teaches education law. Mr. Pattison is a member of the working group of the Children's Rights Litigation Committee of the American Bar Association's Section of Litigation.

**Lourdes M. Rosado** (B.A., Swarthmore College; M.A., Columbia University School of International and Public Affairs; J.D., New York University School of Law; LL.M., Georgetown University Law Center) is associate director of Juvenile Law Center (www.jlc.org) in Philadelphia, Pennsylvania, where she employs a diverse set of strategies to advocate on behalf of children in the foster care and juvenile justice systems. Ms. Rosado pursues civil litigation on behalf of institutionalized children; writes appellate court and amici briefs on key legal issues affecting children involved in public systems; works on legislative and regulatory reform; and trains lawyers and other child-serving professionals on the law. Ms. Rosado joined Juvenile Law Center in 1998 after completing the E. Barrett Prettyman Fellowship in Juvenile Justice at Georgetown University Law Center. Immediately after law school, Ms. Rosado served as a law clerk to the Honorable John R. Padova, United States District Court for the Eastern District of Pennsylvania. Before becoming an attorney, Ms. Rosado worked as a business reporter for *Newsweek* and other publications. Ms. Rosado is currently cochair of the Children's Rights Litigation Committee of the Section of Litigation in the American Bar Association.

**Shari F. Shink** (B.A., University of Pittsburgh; J.D., Rutgers University School of Law) is the founder, executive director for 30 years, and now president emeritus of the Rocky Mountain Children's Law Center. The goal of changing the lives of abused and neglected children has been the guiding mission of Ms. Shink's personal and professional life. A graduate of Rutgers University School of Law in 1975, Ms. Shink began her legal career at Pittsburgh's Child Advocacy Legal Aid Clinic. In 1981, she was recruited by the National Association of Counsel for Children to direct a national demonstration project, the Colorado Guardian *ad litem* Project, and four years later, she launched the Rocky Mountain Children's Law Center. During the 33 years of Ms. Shink's tenure, the Children's Law Center has been a national leader in legal advocacy, education, and public policy reform. Ms. Shink has represented thousands of children and numerous parents, grandparents, and foster parents. A national and international speaker, Ms. Shink inspires others to action on behalf of abused and neglected children and has worked tirelessly to improve Colorado's foster care system. Ms. Shink has successfully challenged barriers in the court and social service systems that have denied children timely decisions, the recognition of psychological parent-child relationships, needed mental health and other services, and permanent and loving families. In addition, Ms. Shink served on Governor Bill Ritter's Child Welfare Action Committee to improve the system in Colorado and, in 2010, spearheaded the development and passage of legislation to create the Child Protection Ombudsman Office, one of the most dramatic and needed reforms in the last three decades. She serves on the working group of the American Bar Association's Section of Litigation's Children's Rights Litigation Committee and is a member of the National Children's Law Network. She assists in the development of children's law centers nationwide and initiated the creation of video training tools on the importance of attorneys for children and methods to interview children that are distributed nationally to judges, attorneys, and law students. Her work has earned her numerous awards, including the American Bar Association's Child Advocate of the Year Award in 2001, the Lewis Hine Award for Service to Children and Youth in 2004, the Women's Bar Association's Raising the Bar Award in 2010, the Denver Rescue Mission's Women Who Have Changed the Heart of the City award in 2013, and the Girl Scouts of Colorado's Women of Distinction award in 2013.

**Casey Trupin** (B.A., Pomona College; J.D., University of Washington School of Law) is the coordinating attorney for the Children and Youth Project at Columbia Legal Services in Seattle, where he advocates for at-risk, homeless, and foster youth. Mr. Trupin has served as counsel to thousands of foster youth and homeless adults in litigation and worked on state and federal legislation designed to improve services to low-income children, youth, and adults in Washington State and nationwide. Mr. Trupin is cochair of the Children's Rights Litigation Committee of the Section of Litigation of the American Bar Association (ABA) and is a special advisor to the ABA's Commission on Homelessness and Poverty, which he chaired from 2006 to 2009. Mr. Trupin co-teaches the Legislative Advocacy Clinic at the University of Washington School of Law, where he previously taught street law. Mr. Trupin has authored or edited numerous books and articles on at-risk, homeless, and foster children, including *Educating Children without Housing: A Primer on Legal Requirements and Implementation Strategies for Educators, Advocates and Policymakers* (3d ed.) (ABA, 2009). In 1997, Mr. Trupin cofounded Street Youth Legal Advocates of Washington (SYLAW) and went on to direct the program until 2005. From 2005 to 2006, Mr. Trupin worked on federal child welfare policy as Counsel for Special Projects at the Center for Law and Social Policy (CLASP) in Washington, D.C. Mr. Trupin has received national recognition for his work, including the ABA's Child Advocacy Award—Distinguished Lawyer (2011), the National Network for Youth's Advocacy Spirit Award (2010), and the Congressional Angel in Adoption Award (2005). From 2006 to 2012, Mr. Trupin served as the inaugural chair of the William H. Gates Public Service Law Program at the University of Washington School of Law.

# FOREWORD

In the early 1990s, I served on the American Bar Association's Working Group on the Unmet Legal Needs of Children and Their Families, whose mission, in part, was to explore ways in which the justice system could better serve children and their families. One of the group's main recommendations was that children should have competent legal counsel to represent them while in the custody of the government. This recommendation has been echoed and re-echoed by many, many children's advocacy groups since that time. Nonetheless, currently throughout the United States, most children who have been taken into custody by the government remain unrepresented by their own lawyer in legal proceedings in which life-altering decisions are made. These decisions include removing them from their homes against their will, excluding them from our public schools, locking them up in psychiatric or detention facilities, placing them in group homes, and deporting them from our country. These children, in many instances, are forced to confront adversarial lawyers alone, without guidance and without the ability to confide in an advisor and advocate whom they can trust.

In dependency proceedings, the state has its lawyers, the child's parents are each entitled to their own lawyer, the foster care agencies have their lawyers and caseworkers, and even the guardian in the Florida *ad litem* program has, inexplicably, its own lawyer in the courtroom, representing not the child but the guardian.

In an immigration court, some children are completely alone and unrepresented when forced to confront a strange and unknown legal system, and one conducted in an alien language.

Denying children a lawyer in all of these circumstances flies in the face of the constitutional guarantee of due process, which demands that every person, including minor children, whose life and liberty are at stake, have an opportunity to be heard. Our judicial system is an adversarial one that really only works when *all* parties are heard and are able to advocate, generally through a lawyer, to ensure the protection of their rights. Moreover, the principle of confidentiality that is at the foundation of the lawyer-client relationship promotes the development of trust that is critical not just to effective lawyering with children but also to viable outcomes in child-centered judicial proceedings. Equally important, many of the few foster children who have been lucky enough to have their own lawyer have expressed the view that just knowing someone was speaking on their behalf enabled them to want to participate and to better accept whatever decisions the court reached.

As *Changing Lives: Lawyers Fighting for Children* aptly demonstrates, lawyers can and do make a positive difference in legal proceedings bearing on a child's life and liberty. Well-trained and experienced lawyers, such as the ones featured in this book, make well-researched and informed arguments on their client's behalf, thereby assisting judges to issue fully informed and thoughtful rulings; hold public agencies accountable for providing the protections and services to which children are entitled under the law; and expedite processes, urging the state and other interested parties to reach and implement resolutions in a timely manner. As the United States Supreme Court noted:

> [N]o single action holds more potential for achieving procedural justice for the child in the juvenile court than provision of counsel. The presence of an independent legal representative of the child, or of his parent, is the keystone of the whole structure of guarantees that a minimum system of procedural justice requires.... The most informal and well intentioned of judicial proceedings are technical; few adults without legal training can influence or even understand them; certainly children cannot.[1]

Although written in the context of juvenile delinquency proceedings, these words are equally applicable when a child is confronted by any aspect of the legal system while in governmental custody. It is lawyers, and only lawyers, who are not only educated and trained, but authorized to advocate

---

1. *In re* Gault, 387 U.S. 1, 39 (1967) (citation omitted).

for and make legal arguments on behalf of another in a judicial proceeding. Although in the case of children, other well-intentioned individuals, such as caseworkers and guardians, purport to speak on behalf of what they perceive to be the best interests of children, only a lawyer who is representing the child is obligated to speak *for* the child, thereby ensuring that the child's due process rights are protected.

The children you will meet in *Changing Lives: Lawyers Fighting for Children* have experienced everything we do not want for them. They have been removed from their homes and separated from their parents and siblings; locked up in poorly run residential and psychiatric facilities and group homes; kicked out of school; forced to live on the streets; and subjected to horrendous physical, sexual, and emotional abuse. But because of the timely intervention and effective advocacy of qualified and dedicated lawyers, these children were able to speak for themselves, to participate fully in the legal proceedings in which they played the central role, and to be assured that all their rights were being protected.

As *Changing Lives: Lawyers Fighting for Children* so well illustrates, one of the most important ways to demonstrate to children that they matter and to ensure better outcomes for youth involved in the legal system is to guarantee that children have a lawyer who will advocate for them at every step of the way.

The Honorable Rosemary Barkett
Arbitrator, Iran-United States Claims Tribunal
Formerly Judge, United States Court of Appeals for the Eleventh Circuit

# INTRODUCTION

Every day in the United States, children have to make decisions. For many children, these choices reflect all the opportunities and resources that our society wishes to make available for each and every youth. Thus, a child may decide to join a school team or write for the student newspaper. A youth may struggle with deciding which parent to invite to Career Day at school or in which family member to confide a problem. Older teenagers try to figure out everything from who to date to what college they will attend. Sometimes the choice is as simple as picking which friend to invite to their house for a sleepover or what movie to see with their older brother.

But other children must make life-altering decisions as a consequence of the dire circumstances in which they find themselves. Hence, a child has to choose whether to stay in an abusive foster home or risk living on the streets. Another child must decide whether to take a guilty plea or go to trial on the criminal charges against him. An immigrant child has to figure out if she should keep quiet about her abusive uncle or say something and take the risk of being deported. For these children, the choices are often between bad and worse.

This book demonstrates the critical role that attorneys play in changing the life courses of our most at-risk children. Without the zealous representation of their attorneys, each of the children profiled in this book likely would have gone down a path that was detrimental to their safety, their well-being, and ultimately their ability to grow into happy and successful adults. *Changing Lives: Lawyers Fighting for Children* well illustrates the difference that a highly trained and skilled attorney can make in the life of a child in need.

Each chapter portrays a real-life case of a child in crisis and describes in detail the lawyering that was brought to bear to achieve the best outcome for that child. In describing these cases, the authors share a wealth of valuable information—including primers on relevant statutory and case law, tips on conducting investigations, advice on utilizing experts, guidance on including social workers and other child-serving professionals on the legal team, and multiple checklists for motions practice and trial advocacy—that will assist practitioners in various areas of the law, including

- child welfare (abuse and neglect)
- juvenile delinquency
- transfer (waiver) from adult criminal court
- immigration
- school discipline
- special education
- mental health
- runaway and homeless youth
- impact litigation to promote systemic reform

The chapters also demonstrate that effectively representing children requires a practitioner to be versed in *multiple* areas of the law. The lawyer who represents a child in a school disciplinary proceeding coordinates with his public defender in his juvenile delinquency case to achieve the best result for the client on both fronts. The lawyer for an immigrant child who is being abused by her caretaker in the United States needs to apply an extensive knowledge of both the child welfare and immigration systems to ensure that the child is removed from her caretaker without being deported. The attorney for a child who has been involuntarily committed for mental health problems advocates for her client to return home by holding the child's school to the requirements of special education laws. By providing inspiring stories combined with practical advice, the authors of *Changing Lives: Lawyers Fighting for Children* hope to raise awareness about the need for legal representation for children and to encourage and support attorneys who advocate for children, both those who do this as a full-time vocation and members of the private bar who undertake pro bono representation.

The attorneys featured in *Changing Lives: Lawyers Fighting for Children* are examples of the best our profession can offer in pursuit of the societal goal of promoting better outcomes for at-risk youth. These attorneys are pioneers, forging new law, pushing the boundaries, and never settling for the self-imposed limits of bureaucracies in their tireless advocacy for their child clients. Unfortunately, too many children who need such zealous advocates at critical turning points in their lives do not have access to them. We are experiencing a crisis in the availability of civil legal and criminal defense services for the indigent and working poor, adults and children alike. Cuts in funding have forced community legal services offices and public defender services to cut staff, increase caseloads to unthinkable numbers, and turn away thousands of people in need of legal representation. It is incumbent on us to stanch the tide by advocating at both the federal and state levels for adequate funding for legal services for the poor, especially children.

There is another key barrier to achieving better outcomes for children that we can overcome without going to our legislatures. It involves a change in attitude. Indeed, perhaps the biggest obstacle to children obtaining quality legal representation is the persistent yet unfounded belief that children simply do not need lawyers. The authors of this volume have heard the comment too often, including from fellow members of the bar, that if courts and agencies just work together in a child's best interest, instead of in the traditional adversarial manner, then the right outcomes will be achieved. The problem is that most of us assume we already know what is in a child's best interest because we may be parents ourselves, and all of us were once children. But these ideas may be based on nothing more than intuition, and we need children's attorneys to challenge these premises if we are to achieve the best result for children. At the end of the day, whether or not you label a proceeding as adversarial, if the parties in the courtroom or at an administrative hearing are represented by counsel, due process demands that the child who is at the center of the proceeding receive no less.

Lourdes M. Rosado

Editor

Cochair, Children's Rights Litigation Committee, Section of Litigation, American Bar Association

# NOTE

The names of all the children described in this book have been changed to protect their identities.

# CHAPTER ONE

## Fighting the Odds
# Speaking for Infants and Toddlers in the Child Welfare System

By Shari F. Shink and Diane Baird

### PART I: GRACE'S STORY

It was December when an attorney with the Support Center for Child Advocates in Philadelphia, Pennsylvania, received a court appointment to represent four-day-old Grace. Grace's birth mother had been involved with the county children and youth agency two years earlier, when she tested positive for cocaine and then gave birth to her first child. After the child's birth, the mother underwent a year of drug and alcohol treatment, as well as mental health treatment. The mother voluntarily relinquished her parental rights to the child, who was subsequently adopted.

Grace's mother was exhibiting mental health issues at the time of Grace's birth. Although she had been on three psychotropic medications, she had stopped taking them during her pregnancy. There were reports of extreme anger and physical altercations. Her erratic behavior led to her eviction from the public shelter system.

At the initial hearing, which the mother attended, all agreed that the goal should be to reunify Grace with her mother. In the meantime, Grace was placed with a foster parent, and her mother was referred to Behavioral Health Services.

Grace's attorney immediately contacted the new foster parent to arrange an initial visit and find out more about the household that baby Grace had joined. During the call, the attorney learned that the foster mother was a single woman who had been a foster parent for a decade and enjoyed taking care of young children. Indeed, the foster mother already had four children under the age of six in her home—a five-year-old developmentally delayed child who was in her permanent custody, and three foster children, two-year-old and three-year-old toddlers and a nine-month-old infant with special medical needs. Baby Grace became the fifth child to join the household. The number and ages of the children in the foster parent's home raised concerns for Grace's attorney. Grace's entry into the foster care system at four days of age should have sounded the alarm for the county children and youth agency to begin concurrent permanency planning. Grace's mother presented with particularly high risks, including long-standing mental health and substance abuse problems, as well as a previous termination of parental rights. Grace's placement, ideally, would have been with a family that could potentially offer permanence.

Grace's attorney quickly called the private foster care agency that had found the placement for Grace. The attorney questioned the number of children in the home, especially given their young ages and special needs, and the home's appropriateness for Grace. The agency representative stated that this foster mother was one of the agency's best and was "on top of everything for the children before being asked." Within a week, Grace's attorney made a home visit. She was concerned about this foster mother because, although loving, she appeared advanced in age. (The attorney later learned that the foster mother was in her mid-seventies.) The permanency goal was reunification with Grace's birth mother, and Grace's attorney remained hopeful that the child would experience only one move before she could return to her birth mother. But Grace's attorney knew that they needed to develop an alternative plan for Grace in case reunification was not possible. Thus, Grace's attorney requested that the county children and youth caseworker attempt to identify and locate the family who had adopted Grace's half brother, to explore whether they might be interested in assuming care of Grace as well. Additionally, she asked that the agency locate the siblings of the man whom the mother had identified as Grace's father, and explore possible placement with them.

Over the next few months, the mother's mental health issues spiraled out of control. She was aggressive and verbally abusive to workers and the foster mother, who took Grace to her supervised visits with her mother. At one visit, the supervising worker heard the mother shouting "I don't want no drugs around!" and "We need security!" The mother also held baby Grace by her feet, tilting her down so that her head almost hit the floor. The visit was immediately stopped.

Grace's attorney advocated for and received an earlier court date to review the matter. While the date was pending, Grace's mother missed three visits with the baby. The mother also filed a missing-persons report on baby Grace; she seemingly was unable to grasp the fact that her child was in foster care, despite the children and youth caseworker's explanations to her. Soon after, the court ordered that all visits stop until Grace's mother could document that she was engaging in mental health treatment. During this same time, the man earlier identified as Grace's possible father was ruled out by paternity testing.

Given that the path to reunification was looking less viable, Grace's attorney focused on Grace's current placement to determine its likely permanence and appropriateness. The attorney again raised concerns about the foster mother as a permanent placement because of her age, but the children and youth caseworker believed that requesting a new home for now four-month-old Grace would be age discrimination. At first, Grace's attorney was ambivalent about pressing the issue. The foster mother was a nice, caring woman who seemed to genuinely love Grace. Over several home visits, the attorney noted affection and good care; the children were provided with good food and shelter, and they all attended timely medical appointments. Yet Grace's attorney did not observe any books, toys, or games, nor did she hear about walks to the park or other outside activities. On most visits, regardless of the time of day, all of the children were still in pajamas. Grace's attorney wanted more for Grace. She wanted play and stimulation; songs and outside activities; opportunities for growth and curiosity. She wanted a loving, active family for Grace.

The children and youth agency scheduled a meeting to set goals and objectives for Grace's case. Meanwhile, more troubling behavior by Grace's mom was observed. In the waiting room, she engaged in a conversation with no one else present. During the meeting, she was aggressive and seemingly out of touch with reality. She angrily claimed to have never given birth to a son who was adopted. She refused to attend drug and alcohol treatment but said she would go to mental health counseling. She agreed she needed medication.

When Grace's attorney next called the foster mother to schedule a visit with Grace, the foster mother told her that both the county children and youth caseworker and the private foster care agency worker had informed her that Grace's attorney wanted Grace removed from her home because of the foster mother's age. Apparently they also shared with the foster mother that they did not agree with Grace's attorney. At the visit, the attorney told the foster parent that while she respected her and appreciated all she was doing for the children in her care, she represented only Grace, now six months old, and her duty was to Grace. Grace's attorney explained that she did not want Grace to lose her birth mother, and then possibly lose an adoptive mom at a young age, which might throw her back into the children and youth system. The foster mother responded that she would be devastated to lose Grace.

In the months before this visit, an appellate case in Pennsylvania indicated that a trial court was not prohibited from allowing one coparenting adult, who did not reside with the biological parent and child, to adopt a child for good cause.[1] Grace's attorney proposed the idea of the foster mother's 50-year-old daughter, who did not live in the home, taking on this coparenting role. When Grace was nine months old, the court raised its own concern over the age of the foster mother and the number of young children in her home. In the next few months, the adult daughter vacillated about whether she was interested in coadopting. Finally, the court gave her two weeks to make a decision, or Grace would be moved. The foster care agency finally reported to the parties that the adult daughter was interested

---

1. *See In re Adoption of J.M.*, 991 A.2d 321 (Pa. Super. Ct. 2010).

in coadopting; however, the adult daughter had not directly expressed this interest to anyone else involved in the case. Grace's attorney needed to hear it directly from the adult daughter herself.

Consequently, Grace's attorney requested a meeting with everyone to discuss the permanency plan. The agency refused to initiate the meeting, so Grace's attorney took the lead and set a meeting for a Saturday morning in the foster mother's home, when the adult daughter was also available. (The foster care worker failed to show up, despite having agreed to the date and time.) At the meeting, Grace's attorney observed a loving relationship between the foster mother's daughter and all of the children and saw their affectionate responses to her. However, it became clear to Grace's attorney that the daughter was ambivalent about the coparenting proposal. She sent mixed messages about her commitment to parenting Grace, such as stating, "I am doing this to save my mother from a broken heart." Moreover, there were concerns that Grace was developmentally slow for her age cohort. Indeed, shortly after this meeting, Grace's pediatrician referred her for an evaluation for language development and motor skills. This was a red flag for Grace's attorney because, based on her many home visits, she knew that Grace lacked appropriate stimulation in the home.

When Grace was fourteen months old, her birth mother's parental rights were finally terminated, a position that Grace's attorney supported, and her permanency goal was changed to adoption. Soon after, another caseworker reported concerns about one of the other children in Grace's foster home. These concerns included inappropriate discipline and a lack of supervision. Subsequently, there was another report, this one concerning Grace, that included neglect and a lack of supervision. Also at this time, the children and youth agency determined that the adult daughter was not really interested in the responsibilities of coparenting Grace. It would only be a co-adoption on paper. Grace's attorney also learned that the family who had adopted Grace's brother was not interested in adopting Grace. Thus, Grace would need to move to a new family for adoption.

When she was 17 months old, Grace was placed with a family newly approved for adoption. Soon, Grace began to thrive and to talk. The observations of Grace's attorney during home visits with the new pre-adoptive family were in sharp contrast to those from visits in the prior foster home.

**5**

Grace was always dressed in "outside" clothes, not pajamas. There were books and toys. Grace's attorney observed Grace taking a book to the pre-adoptive mom and climbing in her lap to be read to. Grace was enrolled in a preschool program twice a week, so that she could play with other children. Grace smiled and laughed.

Within days of placing Grace with this couple, however, the children and youth agency proposed a move for Grace to yet another home. The agency claimed that the pre-adoptive home was only supposed to be a respite home. The couple, however, wanted to keep Grace. And Grace's attorney saw how well the child was adjusting and wanted to minimize moves. At the next court hearing, Grace's attorney requested and received a court order that required that the child not be moved absent an order of the court. Grace's attorney began preparing for a contested "best interests" hearing, while at the same time advocating her position with supervisory agency personnel. Finally, all issues of disagreement were resolved; Grace was not moved again and was adopted by the preadoptive family when she was two years old, after spending her entire life to date in foster care.

One month after Grace's adoption was finalized, Grace's attorney learned that Grace's birth mother had given birth to another baby, out of state. Grace's adoptive family was interested in caring for and ultimately adopting Grace's sibling. Grace's attorney contacted the sibling's out-of-state child advocate and gave him background and identifying information for Grace's family. An interstate compact to pursue adoption in Grace's new home was put in process for her new sibling. This sibling is currently living with Grace and her new family, as is a third child later born to Grace's biological mother.

## PART II: THE CHILD WELFARE SYSTEM

Infants and toddlers represent a distinctive subset of the child welfare population. They have service needs, developmental vulnerabilities, and strengths that distinguish them from other children in out-of-home care.[2]

---

2. Fred Wulczyn, Michelle Ernst & Philip Fisher, *Who Are the Infants in Out-of-Home Care? An Epidemiological and Developmental Snapshot*, CHAPIN HALL ISSUE BRIEF, May 2011, at 1.

Every year, almost 200,000 children from birth to three years of age come into contact with the child welfare system.[3] More than one-third of them are removed from their parents' care,[4] making infants and toddlers the largest single group of children entering foster care.[5] Infants who enter care at less than three months of age are in foster care 50 percent longer than older children and are much more likely to be adopted than reunified with their birth parents.[6]

These young children are at a critical point developmentally. It is during the first years of life that their brains develop at life-altering rates, and they acquire the abilities to think, speak, learn, and reason. Early experiences, both positive and negative, have a decisive effect on how the brain is wired, and it is crucial that we recognize the special vulnerabilities of these young children to developmental harm.[7]

The first relationships that a child forms with adults have the strongest influence on social and emotional development. Indeed, an overarching principle of infant mental health intervention is that relationships are the conduit for change in the young children and families served.[8] Infants and toddlers in foster care face two major problems: the lack of ongoing parent-child contact and, often, multiple moves. Maintaining or healing an attachment with parents is critical for young children but can be difficult, or impossible, while the child is in placement.

Multiple moves while in foster care are a particular concern for infants and toddlers. Transitioning toddlers involves a number of psychological and emotional risks that are specific to this developmental stage. Even very young babies grieve when their relationships are disrupted, and this sadness

---

3. Julie Cohen, Patricia Cole & Jaclyn Szrom, *A Call to Action on Behalf of Maltreated Infants and Toddlers*, ZERO TO THREE (2011), http://www.zerotothree.org/public-policy/federal-policy/childwelfareweb.pdf hereinafter *A Call to Action*, at 2.

4. *Id.*

5. *Id.*

6. Fred Wulczyn et al., *The Foster Care Baby Boom Revisited: What Do the Numbers Tell Us?*, ZERO TO THREE, 31, no. 3 (2011): 4-10, at 4.

7. *A Call to Action*, *supra* note 3, at 3.

8. Brenda Jones Harden, *Infants in the Child Welfare System: Implications for Brain Development* (2012), *webinar available at* http://www.zerotothree.org/public-policy/webinars-conference-calls/jones-harden-website-slides-for-november-17th-webinar.pdf (last visited Sept. 20, 2013).

affects their development. Multiple moves place children at an increased risk for poor outcomes with regard to social-emotional health and the ability to develop healthy attachments.[9] For example, a child's development in the second year of life is driven by the need to explore and master, in concert with the drive to psychologically separate from the dependency of the first year, while maintaining a relationship with the caregiver/parent. Loss of the primary attachment figure during this stage of development is perceived by the child as rejection. This affects the child's sense of safety and confidence in caregivers and the world.[10] The child's developing capacity to regulate emotions, his/her developing sense of self, and his/her capacity to form intimate relationships may all be compromised, temporarily or in the long term.[11]

Research confirms that the early years present an unparalleled window of opportunity to effectively intervene with at-risk children.[12] To be effective, interventions must begin early and be designed with the characteristics and experiences of these infants and toddlers in mind.[13] Child welfare practices must focus on child safety and be structured to promote healthy development and the formation of a secure attachment.[14] Thus, every child welfare decision and service should have a goal of enhancing the well-being of the infant or toddler and his/her family to set the child on a more promising developmental path.[15]

Safety, permanency, and well-being are the three major goals in the Adoption and Safe Families Act of 1997 (42 U.S.C. § 675 et seq.), which is designed to improve outcomes for children in the welfare system. These are the performance measures that child welfare agencies use to measure

---

9. Yvon Gauthier, Gilles Fortin & Gloria Jeliu, *Clinical Application of Attachment Theory in Permanency Planning for Children in Foster Care: The Importance of Continuity of Care,* 25 INFANT MENTAL HEALTH J. 379 (2004).

10. ALICIA F. LIEBERMAN, THE EMOTIONAL LIFE OF THE TODDLER 149–54 (1995).

11. Roger Kobak, *The Emotional Dynamics of Disruptions in Attachment Relationships, in* THE HANDBOOK OF ATTACHMENT THEORY, RESEARCH, AND CLINICAL APPLICATIONS 21 (Jude Cassidy & Philip R. Shaver eds., 2d ed. 1999).

12. *A Call to Action, supra* note 3, at 6.

13. Harden, *supra* note 8.

14. *A Call to Action, supra* note 3, at 6.

15. *Id.*

their own performance and the standards by which the federal government assesses state performance. Because courts in child welfare (dependency) cases are responsible for ensuring that the state is providing proper care to children in its custody, courts need to consider whether these children are physically and emotionally healthy, have permanent relationships, and have families with the capacity to provide for the children's needs.[16]

Grace's case well illustrates that infants and toddlers need strong and vigilant advocates. In the child welfare system, where workers often take the path of least resistance, what is best for a child, especially a nonverbal child, can take a back seat to what is easier for the worker. In Grace's case, the workers advocated for what was best for them as workers—to have Grace stay with a 76-year-old foster mother who appeared to take relatively good care of the child, including taking her for doctor's appointments. Grace may have had adequate care, but not the loving, individualized, and special care she needed to flourish.

Nor did she have a path to permanence with this foster parent in case reunification with the birth mother was not feasible. While Grace's foster mother loved her, she could not provide optimal care or the promise of permanency to Grace. Grace thus built an attachment relationship with an impermanent figure, setting her up for significant loss. Loss affects young children in the same ways that trauma does; it diminishes their trust in the world, their capacity to explore, and their capacity to regulate powerful emotions. The myth that babies forget and recover is false. In fact, their psychological development is shaped by early experience, both positive and negative.[17]

Attorneys owe their allegiance only to the child, not the bureaucratic agencies charged with their care. Children need a lawyer who will advocate zealously only for them; will advocate for their right to be with siblings if possible, no matter how inconvenient; and will push for the best family situation when the child cannot be returned to birth parents. (See Box 1, "Practice Tips for Advocates," and Box 2, "Advocacy at Hearings.")

---

16. Nora E. Sydow & Victor E. Flango, *Physical and Emotional Well-Being: Court Performance Measures for Children and Youth in Foster Care*, Juv. & Fam. Ct. J., Fall 2012, at 1.

17. *A Call to Action, supra* note 3, at 3.

In Grace's case, the attorney advocated for a number of goals that are all crucial to pursuing a good outcome for an infant or toddler in the child welfare system. These included access to family services for Grace's birth mother; visitation between the mother and baby Grace; quality foster care; stability for Grace; the placement of Grace with her siblings; and the legal permanence of adoption. The attorney wisely pursued multiple courses—or concurrent planning—in the event that reunification with the birth mother did not work out. Finally, the attorney knew when to reject reunification as a viable permanency option.

## Access to Family Services

Zealous attorneys for children investigate resources that might benefit the birth family as additions or alternatives to those identified by the child welfare agency. Private community-based agencies, volunteer or donated services, and mentors are options to consider. Mentoring, especially by mothers previously involved in the system who successfully had their children returned to them, may be particularly effective. In Grace's case, her mother's mental health issues left the mother with little capacity to engage in or follow through with needed treatment. In other situations, services might make a critical difference for reunification.

## Visitation

Visitation for infants and toddlers should be as frequent as possible (e.g., daily or multiple times per week) and be conducted in homelike settings that are familiar to the child.[18] Typical child welfare agency policy dictates once-per-week visits between parent and child. In Grace's case, her mother was incapable of meaningful visitation and even presented a dangerous risk, which appropriately led to the temporary cessation of visits. (See Box 3, "Possible Motions in Dependency Court.") Attorneys must be vigilant in staying current with parent-child activities and act when necessary to reduce, change, enhance, or stop visits, as the situation warrants.

---

18. Harden, *supra* note 8.

> **Practice Tip:** If visits pose a risk to the child, the attorney can file a Motion to Terminate Visitations, and attach affidavits. Conversely, if visitation is inappropriately denied, an attorney can file a Motion to Increase Visits.

Unless parental visitation is determined to be detrimental to the child, the visitation plan should specify the frequency and type of contact by the parents, as appropriate. At a minimum, the visitation plan should facilitate and support the following interests and needs of the child:

- the growth and development of the child
- the child's adjustment to the placement
- the foster parent's ability to meet the child's needs
- the child's contacts with parents, siblings, and other family members
- the child's permanency plan

## Quality of Foster Home Placement

Grace's attorney had to balance competing concerns—the quality of the foster care placement versus Grace's need for stability. She was vigilant about visiting her client frequently to continually assess whether and how well Grace's needs were being met. She did not leave that job to the agency. Grace's attorney raised questions about the number of children in the home and the age of the foster mother. She observed activities and patterns, and engaged in many conversations to learn about her client and the care she was receiving. When she began to identify Grace's unmet needs, she moved quickly to determine alternative long-term options for Grace. She explored—and urged the agency to investigate—such options as coparenting by the foster mother's adult daughter and possible placement with Grace's brother's adoptive family.

## Stability

Stability is a critical aspect of permanency and well-being. Ensuring stability targets the continuity of a child's relationships, as well as her environment.

Generally, any action that disrupts or threatens to disrupt stability should be discouraged and challenged.

Stability is especially critical for babies and toddlers. One of the guiding principles that Grace's attorney followed in her advocacy was that Grace's only move ideally should be a return to her birth mother or to an adoptive family, if the foster mother could not provide permanence. Grace's attorney explored the innovative coparenting idea as a way to maintain stability with a family who was already caring for her. When this option and adoption by Grace's brother's adoptive family were determined to be unavailable for Grace, her attorney pursued an adoptive family. A family was found, a transition took place to ease Grace into the new home, and Grace adjusted well and thrived.

Yet Grace's stability was still at risk when the county children and youth agency threatened another move. Not satisfied with the vague reasons offered for the move, and having confirmed through her own investigation that Grace was doing well in the preadoptive family, Grace's attorney actively worked to stop the move. She then requested an evidentiary hearing to present evidence regarding Grace's best interests. The hearing became unnecessary when Grace's attorney successfully persuaded the children and youth agency to maintain Grace's placement with the adoptive family. However, absent the willingness of Grace's attorney to challenge the arbitrary decision making, Grace's adoptive placement would have been disrupted, much to Grace's detriment.

A child should not be moved from one short-term emergency placement to another unless all reasonable efforts to return the child to his/her birth parent's home, or to place the child in a more permanent setting, have been exhausted and are documented.

Moves between levels of care require a court's findings of fact and must be scrutinized to ensure that the resulting placement is the least restrictive and the most appropriate. Once a child is facing a third move, the attorney for the child should request an evidentiary hearing and findings of fact to establish the reason for the move and how the move advances the child's permanency goal. The attorney should advocate for a clearly identified and realistic plan for permanency, and press the court to include the plan in its order.

> **Practice Tip:** All moves should advance permanency. Those that do not must be challenged, and attorneys should request an emergency hearing. Attorneys should oppose administrative moves for licensing issues or agency rules; lateral moves within the same general level of care; and any temporary move from an initial placement, unless to a permanent home.

## Placing Siblings Together

Grace's attorney appropriately explored a sibling placement which ultimately was not available to Grace. Her attorney went an additional mile by contacting the out-of-state attorney for a later-born sibling to suggest that Grace's adoptive family would be interested in the new baby as well. Sibling relationships can give children context and a sense of history, particularly when these relationships have been enduring.[19]

## When to Reject Reunification as an Option

In Grace's case, reunification remained the permanency goal until Grace's mother demonstrated that she could not sufficiently overcome her substance abuse and mental health challenges. In rare circumstances—when there is a severe and chronic history of emotional or mental illness, the previous death of a sibling, serious bodily injury, or pattern of habitual abuse—an attorney may want to urge the court to find "aggravated circumstances" early in the case and hold that the child welfare agency does not have to make "reasonable efforts" to reunify the family but may instead pursue another permanency goal for the child.[20] Such situations may present a persistent inability to parent, and therefore a reunification plan would only subject the child to needless delay, insecurity, and multiple moves.

Alternatively, an attorney could seek a reunification plan with intensive family and other services on a much shorter time line—for example, three

---

19. David J. Whelan, *Using Attachment Theory When Placing Siblings in Foster Care*, 20 CHILD & ADOLESCENT SOC. WORK J. 21 (2003).

20. ASFA allows states to define and clarify what acts by the birth parents constitute aggravated circumstances. 45 C.F.R. § 1356.21(b)(3) (2012).

months to make meaningful progress—and advocate for a concurrent plan for immediate placement of the child in a legal-risk home, that is, a foster home willing to parent temporarily, and adopt when the child is legally freed for adoption. This would give the parent the opportunity to demonstrate progress that was dramatically different from his/her past history while minimizing instability for the child.

## Permanence

There is widespread and general acknowledgement among behavioral scientists, pediatricians, psychologists and others that emotional and cognitive disruptions in the early lives of children have the potential to impair brain development.[21] Paramount in the lives of children in foster care is their need for continuity in their relationships with their primary attachment figures and a sense of permanence. Expediting permanency requires a sense of urgency for young children (and their siblings), but all children need stability. As Chief Justice Michael Bender of the Colorado Supreme Court has stated, all children who have been removed from their homes are guaranteed a new home where they "can feel safe and secure, they will not arbitrarily be removed from those homes, and they can, if appropriate, confidently plan for their future."[22]

Permanency must be considered at the earliest stages of a case. In promoting this goal, a child's attorney should expedite assessments of the child to determine unmet needs. To accomplish this, attorneys can

- file motions for medical and/or mental health evaluations and ensure implementation of treatment recommendations;
- ensure that the child is provided with a full medical examination (within two weeks of receiving appointment) and full dental examination (within eight weeks) and maintain regularly scheduled appointments as recommended;[23]

---

21. Roberta Hibbard *et al.*, *Psychological Maltreatment*, PEDIATRICS 2012;130;372, available at http://pediatrics.aappublications.org/content/130/2/372.full.html.
22. City of Northglenn v. Ibarra, 62 P.3d 151, 160 (Colo. 2003).
23. *See, e.g.*, Colo. Dep't of Hum. Serv., Vol. 7, 7.304.62 (G).

- seek other state or county funding sources if a medical, dental, or psychological evaluation is necessary and cannot be covered under Medicaid or third-party insurance;
- consider and explore trauma-informed treatment at the earliest stages;[24]
- advocate that any assessment, whether formal or informal, of families being considered as a permanent home should be completed in the earliest stages of the case.

* * *

Representing infants and toddlers offers a unique opportunity to significantly impact the life and future of a child. Grace's case demonstrates the disastrous outcomes lying in wait for a child without zealous advocacy. Early intervention for positive outcomes sets the foundation for quality learning experiences, mental and physical health, nurturing relationships, and, ultimately, success in the world. As a society, we will share these children's success, and the impact will be felt for generations.

---

24. *See, e.g.,* Bruce D. Perry & Erin P. Hambrick, *The Neurosequential Model of Therapeutics*, RECLAIMING CHILD. & YOUTH, Fall 2008, at 39.

## Box 1: Practice Tips for Advocates

- First and foremost, know your client.
- Be bold and courageous. Imagine this child is your own.
- Do an independent investigation. For example, learn about felony convictions of foster/relative placements.
- Pursue placement alternatives for your client. It is not just the agency's job. Explore placements that will keep siblings together and keep children local. In many states, the court is not bound by county rules and regulations. Where an appropriate placement for your client, such as with a schoolteacher or family friend, is not licensed, seek a court order or parental permission for the placement.
- Look to neighbors, teachers, and others with whom the child has a relationship, and seek foster care or kinship funding for these caregivers. Some states have sought and received federal waivers to use discretionary funding to support nonfamily placements to better serve children.
- Keep in mind that as the child's attorney, you have numerous opportunities to persuade the court to enter orders that may be different or unusual, but uniquely appropriate to your individual client and within the court's broad discretion.
- Once a child is facing a third move (more than the national average), advocate for extraordinary measures, such as weekly court reviews, to pressure the actors to find a permanent home.
- Engage experts to assist in ensuring the right outcome for your client as well as to educate the court. Experts can provide input by phone, by affidavit, or in person. Fly in a national expert when necessary. Many donors to nonprofit agencies willingly donate miles for air travel. Many hotels will eagerly donate a hotel room for a good cause.

## Box 2: Advocacy at Hearings

- Convey a sense of urgency at every hearing; children grow quickly, developmental windows close, and opportunities end.
- Seek deadlines in the court orders for needed evaluations, treatment, and other services.
- Insist on accountability of all parties.
- Cite legal authority. Be ready to give the judge a copy of the case or statute.
- Quote the American Academy of Pediatrics and other national experts on child development.
- Quote experts from your own case (e.g., the mental health evaluator, counselor, parenting coordinator, early intervention specialist).
- Make offers of proof to avoid long hearings or delays, and use affidavits when appropriate.
- Request hearings on Saturdays or evenings to respond to emergencies.

## Box 3: Possible Motions in Dependency Court

- Motion for Emergency Hearing: Appropriate when the child's attorney does not receive notice of and/or objects to a placement change.
- Motion to Return Child to Placement: Appropriate when a child is removed without notice to and/or consent of the child's attorney. The child's attorney also should seek an order to pay for immediate treatment to address trauma caused by the move. (In one jurisdiction, the court ordered the department to provide treatment for an 18-month-old child removed without a court order, and ordered that the treatment continue until his 18th birthday.)
- Motion to Prevent Removal of Child Due to Attachment with Foster Family or Relative.
- Motion to Require Placement of Siblings Together.
- Motion for Visitation between Siblings (while separated).
- Motion to Evaluate Caregiver-Child Relationship.
- Motion for Immediate Trauma-Informed Treatment for Child.
- Motions for Normative Opportunities/Experiences to Stabilize Placement. These can include sports, recreational activities, artistic activities, and other extracurricular activities and should be considered in every case.

# CHAPTER TWO

### Letting Children Be Children
# Advocating for Youth in the Juvenile Justice System

By Lourdes M. Rosado with Candace Mitchell

### PART I: MARCUS'S STORY

When the discovery of an apparent explosive in the hallways of a Washington, D.C., middle school became headline news, 13-year-old Marcus found himself at the center of a storm. One Saturday, the precocious, baby-faced teen, who had an avid interest in science, did an experiment in the apartment he shared with his mother. He had seen someone on television make a Molotov cocktail, or a gasoline bomb, and decided to create his own. Marcus poured household products he found under the sink—pine cleanser, bleach, and stainless steel cleaner—into an empty liquor bottle he had picked up on the street, attached a wick made of toilet paper, and taped up his creation to add a flair of authenticity. Knowing his mom would get mad if anything leaked out on her white carpet, he threw the bottle in his backpack and forgot all about it.

But when Marcus went to school the next Monday and passed through a metal detector, he roused the suspicion of a security guard who saw the bottle in his backpack. School officials then conducted a search of Marcus's locker, where they found a lighter in a coat pocket. The school alerted the Metropolitan Police Department and the D.C. Fire Department, and officials descended on the school to investigate. Despite the fact that Marcus didn't socialize with other kids and hadn't talked to anyone that morning, a few students claimed that Marcus had said he was going to blow up the school. The school responded by holding an all-school assembly, which only fanned the gossip and innuendo. Pretty soon, word got out to the media. Local newspapers and television crews reported that a student had been arrested for bringing an "explosive device" to school and that school officials were calling for his immediate expulsion.

By the end of the day, an adolescent mistake born out of curiosity and boredom had transformed into a crime that was all over the news. Marcus was immediately suspended from school and threatened with expulsion; arrested and charged with a battery of offenses, including felony arson; and locked up in detention. For the first time in his young life, Marcus was in trouble—serious trouble—and in need of a lawyer.

Fortunately, Marcus's sister found him a legal team—a group of attorneys, fellows, interns, and investigators in the Juvenile Justice Clinic at the Georgetown University Law Center. Marcus's sister knew the Juvenile Justice Clinic's director, Kristin Henning, through her collaboration with a teen group that used art to combat city violence; she recognized Ms. Henning in the courthouse hallway while awaiting her brother's initial hearing. Marcus and his family soon presented the clinic with an adamant, and seemingly impossible, request: that Marcus come out of the incident with no delinquency record that the public could see. Marcus's legal team knew that the request meant they would have to be prepared to take his case to trial and that they would need to invest an extraordinary amount of time in relationship-building, research, and investigation.

The judge at the initial hearing balked at the felony arson charge, the most serious offense that Marcus faced, telling prosecutors that they were "ridiculous" to think that they could prove arson based on the evidence he had heard; specifically, the judge doubted that they could prove an essential element of the crime absent any actual attempt by Marcus to burn property. But the high visibility of the case put pressure on the prosecutors to pursue the stiffest charges against Marcus. Marcus's attorneys successfully advocated that Marcus be released from detention to await trial. Although the judge at the initial hearing allowed the case to go forward, he rejected the government's request to put an electronic monitor on Marcus and instead put Marcus under intensive probation supervision. However, juvenile probation put an electronic monitor on Marcus in defiance of the court's order. When Marcus later appeared in court with an electronic monitor on his leg, his defense counsel quickly made a successful motion to the court to have it removed.

Marcus's defense team engaged in intense discovery and investigation from the first day, including subpoenaing Marcus's school documents as well as interviewing students, teachers, and counselors. Picking up on the court's cue that the prosecution had an uphill battle in proving arson, Marcus's attorneys secured funds from the court to hire a fire expert. In the process, Marcus's lawyers also became quasi fire experts themselves, digesting masses of scientific literature. Based on what Marcus had said about what he put into the bottle, the fire expert doubted that Marcus had created a flammable liquid; while stainless steel cleaner may be flammable alone, the other products would have diluted it so that it could not be set on fire. But the expert said he needed to test the liquid himself, so his defense team requested that the government produce it at a discovery meeting. Much to their surprise, crime scene investigators showed up with an empty bottle— officials had failed to preserve the contents. Marcus's attorneys immediately filed a motion to dismiss the petition for failure to preserve the liquid. The defense team presented evidence at the motion hearing establishing that the D.C. Fire Department response team—which had poured the contents of the bottle down a drain before leaving the school—had not followed their internal guidelines or national fire protection standards, which the defense's fire expert had provided. Nevertheless, the court found that the response team's actions were reasonable and denied the defense motion. Marcus's defense team prepared to go to trial.

Meanwhile, Marcus's court case was not his only problem. He was suspended from school and facing expulsion. Upon accepting the case, Marcus's lawyers immediately called the Juvenile and Special Education Law Clinic of the David A. Clarke School of Law at the University of the District of Columbia (UDC) to represent Marcus in his school discipline case. The UDC clinic leapt into action. Since Marcus was a special education student, the UDC clinic requested a review meeting to determine whether Marcus's behavior was a manifestation of his disability, as well as an administrative

**21**

review hearing to challenge the merits of the suspension and proposed expulsion. The UDC clinic successfully argued that school officials had committed a procedural violation in suspending Marcus, and the hearing officer ordered that Marcus be allowed back in school. Later, the UDC clinic established that Marcus's conduct in bringing the bottle to school was a "manifestation" of his disability under special education law. As a result, Marcus stayed in school and finished the rest of the academic year without incident. The hearing officer also granted Marcus compensatory education in the form of tutoring to help him catch up and re-engage in school.

Back in court, the trial date approached, and the government offered an unexpected plea: the felony charges would be dropped and Marcus could plead guilty to a misdemeanor that would not show up in his public record. Marcus entered a plea, but his lawyers then pushed the case even further—they filed on the spot a 20-page motion to dismiss the case in the interest of justice. (A District of Columbia statute that exists in few other jurisdictions allows a court to dismiss a delinquency case in the interest of justice.) Marcus's attorneys had known from the start of their representation how important it was to keep Marcus out of detention and in school while he was awaiting trial. Indeed, that was one of the key reasons why they enlisted the UDC clinic to represent Marcus in his school discipline and special education cases. Marcus's attorneys presented evidence at the plea hearing of Marcus's excellent school attendance and performance, including awards he had won; his involvement with various after school, volunteer, mentoring, and church groups; and his compliance with all probation terms, which had prompted the probation department to support the dismissal. The lawyers won the motion and the case was dismissed.

## PART II: REPRESENTING YOUTH IN THE JUVENILE JUSTICE SYSTEM

A group of attorneys who specialize in representing youth came to Marcus's aid and helped him successfully navigate what could have been a life-altering event. As a result of nine months of work by a dedicated team, Marcus does not have a delinquency record at all. Instead of being locked up in a correctional facility, Marcus now attends his neighborhood public school, which provides him with accommodations that meet his special

**22**

needs while he pursues his interest in science. But other children in Marcus's position may not be so fortunate, because they may not have access to attorneys who have the time and resources and who are especially trained to represent children.

In 1967, the United States Supreme Court held in *In re Gault* that children have a constitutional right to counsel in delinquency proceedings.[1] Despite this landmark ruling, we still see too many instances in which children facing charges do not get lawyers, or are pressured to waive counsel. The Luzerne County, Pennsylvania, juvenile court corruption scandal that broke in 2009 was one of the most highly publicized recent examples of such violations of due process. Two judges were convicted of taking $2.9 million in kickbacks from the developer and co-owner of private, for-profit detention facilities in which the judges placed thousands of youth. An investigation by a special master found that in a five-year period, thousands of youth were adjudicated delinquent without representation by attorneys. A 2010 report by the American Civil Liberties Union of Wyoming and the National Center for Youth Law told of children in Wyoming as young as eight years old being criminally prosecuted in adult courts for typical child and adolescent misbehavior such as stealing a pack of gum, skateboarding in the wrong place, smoking at school, or drinking at a weekend party.[2] In fact, investigators observed during site visits that only a few of the children who entered guilty pleas were represented by counsel.[3]

And in too many jurisdictions, children charged with delinquency offenses are pressured to waive counsel and plead guilty to charges without the benefit of a lawyer's assistance. "We know from careful national studies that juveniles who lack counsel are much more likely to plead guilty without offering any defense or mitigating evidence," explains Laurence H. Tribe, professor of law at Harvard Law School and former senior counsel for

1. *In re Gault*, 387 U.S. 1 (1967).
2. PAT ARTHUR & MIKAELA RABINOWITZ, NAT'L CTR. FOR YOUTH LAW, & JENNIFER HORVATH, ACLU, WYO. CHAPTER, A CALL TO STOP CHILD PROSECUTIONS IN WYOMING ADULT COURTS 2 (2010).
3. *Id.* at 20.

Access to Justice, U.S. Department of Justice.[4] Tribe, who is alarmed by the trend of children forgoing representation by counsel, has noted that young people who lack counsel "are far more likely to end up in detention or incarceration, where they're much more likely to be exposed to assault or sexual abuse, much more vulnerable to suicide, and far more likely to commit further crimes after their release."[5]

Law enforcement agencies arrested approximately 1.9 million youth under the age of 18 in the United States in 2009, the most recent year for which data is available.[6] Less than 5% of the arrests were for violent crimes.[7] (In fact, between 1994—when the Violent Crime Index arrest rates for juveniles hit a historic high—and 2009, that rate fell nearly 50% to its lowest level since at least 1980.[8]) By contrast, 22% of the 2009 arrests were for property crimes.[9] About 1.5 million of the 2009 arrests ended up in juvenile court, which means that juvenile courts processed 49 cases for every 1,000 youth under 18 in the general population.[10] About one-third of the court cases resulted in a delinquency adjudication, the juvenile court equivalent of a conviction.[11] A juvenile court judge typically sits as the fact-finder in these adjudicatory hearings, as youth in juvenile court do not have a constitutional right to trial by a jury of their peers.[12]

Upon adjudicating a child delinquent, the court may choose from a wide range of disposition—or sentencing—options, ranging from community service and probation to the most restrictive, removal from home and placement in a public or private correctional facility. In 2009, juvenile courts ordered out-of-home placement in 27% of all cases adjudicated

---

4. Laurence H. Tribe, Keynote Remarks at the Annual Conference of Chief Justices (July 26, 2010), http://www.justice.gov/atj/opa/pr/speeches/2010/atj-speech-100726.html.

5. *Id.*

6. CHARLES PUZZANCHERA & BENJAMIN ADAMS, OFF. OF JUV. JUST. & DELINQUENCY, JUVENILE ARRESTS 2009 4 (2011).

7. *See id.*

8. *See* JEFFREY A. BUTTS, JOHN JAY COLL. OF CRIM. JUST., VIOLENT YOUTH CRIME PLUMMETS TO A 30-YEAR LOW (2012).

9. *See* PUZZANCHERA & ADAMS, *supra* note 6, at 4.

10. CHARLES PUZZANCHERA, BENJAMIN ADAMS & SARAH HOCKENBERRY, NAT'L CTR. FOR JUV. JUST., JUVENILE COURT STATISTICS 2009 6, 8 (2012).

11. *See id.* at 6, 46.

12. McKeiver v. Pennsylvania, 403 U.S. 528, 545 (1971).

delinquent, translating into approximately 133,800 youth being taken from their homes.[13] On any given night, about 60,500 youth are in some type of out-of-home placement by order of a delinquency court.[14] About 40% of these youth are in large, locked-down facilities, which closely resemble adult prisons, complete with barbed wire and isolation cells.[15] This is in addition to roughly 25,000 youth held daily in detention centers, either awaiting trial or pending placement in a correctional program.[16] The U.S. youth incarceration rate is far higher than that of any other nation, despite studies that show that U.S. youth released from correctional facilities recidivate at higher rates as compared to their noninstitutionalized peers.[17] In addition to being ineffective, mass incarceration of youth is expensive, costing states $88,000 to lock up a youth for one year.[18]

There were 74.1 million youth under 18 in the U.S. population in 2010.[19] Astonishingly, almost one-half that number—or 31 million youth—were under some type of juvenile court jurisdiction in 2009.[20] In many respects, Marcus fit the profile of the typical youth who gets caught up in the justice system—he was a young African American male being raised by a single mother in a housing project while his father was incarcerated. Moreover, Marcus had learning disabilities and Attention Deficit Hyperactivity Disorder (ADHD) and was arrested for something that allegedly happened at school. Minority children—particularly black youth—are disproportionally represented at all stages of the juvenile justice system. In 2009, the racial composition of the U.S. juvenile population ages 10–17 was 77% white, 16% black, 5% Asian/Pacific Islander, and 1% American Indian.[21]

---

13. PUZZANCHERA, ADAMS & HOCKENBERRY, *supra* note 10, at 51, 58.
14. ANNIE E. CASEY FOUND., NO PLACE FOR KIDS: THE CASE FOR REDUCING JUVENILE INCARCERATION 2 (2011). This number is from 2007, the most recent data available.
15. *Id.*
16. *Id.*
17. *Id.* at 2–3.
18. *Id.* at 19.
19. CHILD TRENDS DATA BANK, NUMBER OF CHILDREN 3 (2013), http://www.childtrends.org/wp-content/uploads/2012/07/53_Number_of_Children.pdf.
20. PUZZANCHERA, ADAMS & HOCKENBERRY, *supra* note 10, at 8. Of these youth, 79% were between the ages of 10 and 15, 12% were age 16, and 9% were age 17. *Id.*
21. PUZZANCHERA & ADAMS, *supra* note 6, at 6. Most juveniles of Hispanic ethnicity were included in the white racial category.

By contrast, juvenile arrests for violent crimes in 2009 were 47% white, 51% black, 1% Asian, and 1% American Indian. For property crime arrests, the proportions were 64% white, 33% black, 2% Asian, and 1% American Indian youth.[22] That same year, the total delinquency case rate—the number of cases processed in juvenile court per 1,000 youth in the population—for black juveniles was more than double the rate for white and American Indian juveniles.[23] In fact, for all years between 1985 and 2009, formal processing—as opposed to informal diversion—was more likely for cases of black youth than those involving white youth.[24] Indeed, the mass incarceration of African American men in the United States has led at least one commentator to call this the "new Jim Crow" era.[25]

Like Marcus, a significant percentage of court-involved children have learning disabilities and Individualized Education Plans, or IEPs, under federal special education law. Youth in the juvenile justice population are more likely than those in the general population to be diagnosed with learning disabilities, emotional disturbance, mental retardation, and speech or language impairments.[26] Different theories are posited for why youth with disabilities are overrepresented in the juvenile court. The differential treatment theory hypothesizes that because juvenile justice stakeholders do not understand that certain youth characteristics and behaviors may be linked to a disability, they may treat disabled youth more harshly than their nondisabled peers for comparable behavior.[27] The metacognitive deficit theory posits that because youth with disabilities have poorer problem-solving strategies, they are more likely to engage in delinquent behavior.[28]

And like Marcus, children formally processed in the juvenile court are more likely to be from low-income families as opposed to families in the

---

22. *Id.*
23. PUZZANCHERA, ADAMS & HOCKENBERRY, *supra* note 10, at 20.
24. *Id.* at 39.
25. *See generally* MICHELLE ALEXANDER, THE NEW JIM CROW: MASS INCARCERATION IN THE AGE OF COLORBLINDNESS (2010).
26. PETER LEONE ET AL., SPECIAL EDUCATION AND DISABILITY RIGHTS, MODULE 3 OF TOWARD DEVELOPMENTALLY APPROPRIATE PRACTICE: A JUVENILE COURT TRAINING CURRICULUM, at 1–2 (Nat'l Juv. Defender Ctr. & Juv. Law Ctr. ed., 2009).
27. *Id.* at 3.
28. *Id.* at 3–4.

middle and upper income brackets. As Tamar Birckhead points out, the critical role that children's socioeconomic status plays in propelling them into the juvenile courts has yet to be fully studied and tracked as compared to factors of race and ethnicity.[29] But what little data is available confirms the prevalence of poor children in the system.[30] Birckhead further argues that the disproportionate adjudication of poor children may occur because courts will act to provide services to address the perceived needs of the individual child, as opposed to simply considering whether the evidence establishes beyond a reasonable doubt that the child committed the alleged offense.[31] In other words, courts may be less interested in whether a child is guilty or innocent and instead may adjudicate a child delinquent in order to get him or her services that the court perceives the child to need but that the family may be unable to afford.[32]

Marcus's case also illustrates another trend in juvenile justice—children being arrested for offenses that allegedly happened at school. Since the mid-1990s, "zero tolerance" policies have made public schools a major feeder of youth into the juvenile courts.[33] (See the chapter "Staying on Track: Protecting Youth in School Discipline Actions," which discusses school discipline and zero tolerance policies.) The child welfare system is another feeder into the juvenile delinquency court that contributes to the problem of disproportionate minority representation. A high percentage of youth who enter the foster care system because of abuse or neglect "cross over"

---

29. Tamar R. Birckhead, *Delinquent by Reason of Poverty*, 38 WASH. U. J.L. & POL'Y 53, 58 (2012).

30. *See id.* at 58–59 ("Although few juvenile courts formally keep track of the income-level of a youth's family, jurisdictions that do so have confirmed that nearly sixty percent were either on public assistance or had annual incomes of less than twenty thousand dollars. Another twenty percent had incomes of less than thirty thousand dollars.").

31. *Id.* at 61; *see also id.* at Part III generally.

32. *Id.* at 59.

33. Advancement Project, *Test, Punish, and Push Out: How "Zero Tolerance" and High Stakes Testing Funnel Youth into the School-to-Prison Pipeline* 29 (2010), http://www.advancementproject.org/resources/entry/test-punish-and-push-out-how-zero-tolerance-and-high-stakes-testing-funnel.

into the juvenile justice system.[34] Indeed, children of color in the child welfare system are twice as likely to be arrested as their white counterparts.[35]

Marcus is representative of other African American males who become entangled in the juvenile court in that he was detained, albeit for only one night, in a detention facility. While black youth represented 34% of the juvenile court cases in 2009, they made up 42% of the detention caseload.[36] After adjudication, the likelihood of out-of-home placement in 2009 was greater for black youth (31%) and American Indian youth (29%) than for white (25%) or Asian youth (23%).[37] Thanks to Marcus's strong family support and the aggressive advocacy by his defense team, Marcus was spared the trauma of being removed from his home and locked up. Studies document that youth in correctional facilities are often subject to pervasive violence and physical and sexual abuse.[38]

Even if not placed outside the home, adjudicated youth must contend with serious collateral consequences well into their adulthood. "The consequences of juvenile adjudications are serious and long term; the lack of representation can reshape a child's entire life," explains Tribe.[39] "Being found guilty can mean expulsion from school, exclusion from the job market, eviction from public housing, and exclusion from the opportunity to enlist in the military. It can affect immigration status."[40] Indeed, the American Bar Association launched the Think before You Plead project to better inform youth, parents, and advocates about the collateral consequences of a juvenile delinquency adjudication.[41]

The lawyering in Marcus's case demonstrates the diverse skills and expertise needed to zealously represent youth charged with crimes. To begin, such

34. FED. ADVISORY COMM. ON JUV. JUST., ANNUAL REPORT 2010, at 3–4 (2010), *available at* http://www.facjj.org/annualreports/00-FACJJ%20Annual% 20Report-FINAL%20508.pdf; *see generally* Shay Bilchik & Michael Nash, *Child Welfare and Juvenile Justice: Two Sides of the Same Coin*, JUV. & FAM. JUST. TODAY 16 (Fall 2008).

35. Bilchik & Nash, *supra* note 34, at 17.

36. PUZZANCHERA, ADAMS & HOCKENBERRY, *supra* note 10, at 33.

37. *Id.* at 53.

38. NO PLACE FOR KIDS, *supra* note 14, at 5–9.

39. Tribe, *supra* note 4.

40. *Id.*

41. AM. BAR ASS'N, THINK BEFORE YOU PLEAD: JUVENILE COLLATERAL CONSEQUENCES IN THE UNITED STATES, http://www.beforeyouplea.com/ (last visited July 12, 2013).

lawyers must litigate the same issues as do criminal defense attorneys, and they must be well versed in the rules of criminal procedure, discovery, and evidence. Marcus's lawyers obtained his release from pre-trial detention and successfully moved to take him off of electronic monitoring, thus decreasing his odds of being adjudicated delinquent. Their investigation and work with a fire expert led them to request the contents of the bottle to test if it was indeed flammable. (See Box 1, "Investigation Checklist," and Box 2, "Expert Checklist.") And the team later argued a motion to dismiss for the government's failure to preserve key evidence. (See Box 3, "Motions Practice.") It is also likely that the prosecution's plea offer stemmed in part from the defense team's zealous advocacy, and the plea was followed by the defense team's successful motion to dismiss the entire case.

Attorneys who represent youth in juvenile court go beyond the role of the traditional criminal defense attorney. Such lawyers must contend with collateral matters that arise with, or as a result of, their client's juvenile court involvement. In Marcus's case, that meant securing attorneys to represent him in the school suspension/expulsion proceedings. Marcus's lawyers knew how critical it is to keep youth in regular schools and out of alternative schools, which tend to have poor standards and curriculum. Moreover, unlike criminal convictions, a delinquency adjudication in most states is a two-step process: first, a fact finding that the youth committed the alleged act; and second, a finding that the child is in need of a program of treatment, or rehabilitation. That means that delinquency attorneys have another avenue to avoid adjudication—to show that a child is not in need of such a program. In Marcus's case, his legal team needed to convince the judge that the child whom the media and prosecutors portrayed as a maladjusted arsonist with a gripe and a bomb was really a bright kid with curiosity and adolescent shortsightedness. They were able to do this in large part by keeping him in his school, where he finished the rest of the academic year without incident.

In one key respect, Marcus's case was not typical of what other youth experience when they become entangled with the juvenile justice system—he had access to trained attorneys who had the time and resources to provide him with zealous representation. In marking the 50th anniversary of *Gideon v. Wainwright*[42] in 2013, the landmark U.S. Supreme Court case that preceded *Gault* and established the right to counsel for adults facing criminal prosecution, legal commentators pointed to the current crisis in indigent defense, as understaffed and underresourced public defender offices carry overwhelming caseloads.[43] Unless we address this crisis, children such as Marcus will be driven into the justice system, at great cost not only to the children themselves but to society as a whole.

## Box 1: Investigation Checklist

- Get written permission from your client to collect information about him/her.
- Conduct a thorough, critical client interview.
- Meet with all potential defense witnesses.
- Make a witness chart.
- Look into the client's court history.
- Look into the client's social history.
- Visit the crime scene.
- Collect physical evidence and other relevant information.
- Hire forensic experts to do analysis of evidence.
- Attempt to interview adverse witnesses.

*Adapted from* ELIZABETH CALVIN, SARAH MARCUS, GEORGE OLEYER & MARY ANN SCALI, NAT'L JUV. DEFENDER CTR., JUVENILE DEFENDER DELINQUENCY NOTEBOOK 93–97 (2006).

---

42. Gideon v. Wainwright, 372 U.S. 335 (1963).
43. Mark Walsh, *Fifty Years after Gideon, Lawyers Still Struggle to Provide Counsel to the Indigent*, A.B.A. J., Mar. 1, 2013, http://www.abajournal.com/magazine/article/fifty_years _after_gideon_lawyers_still_struggle_to_provide_counsel.

## Box 2: Expert Checklist

Some of the most commonly used experts in juvenile delinquency cases include the following:

- Fingerprint examiners
- Ballistics experts
- Narcotics and drug experts
- A variety of mental health experts, including psychiatrists, psychologists, and neurologists
- Handwriting experts and questioned-document examiners
- Arson experts
- Shoeprint/tire tread experts
- Polygraph examiners
- Serologists (to analyze blood, urine, saliva, semen, and other bodily fluids)
- Forensic pathologists
- Hair and fiber examiners

*Adapted from* RANDY HERTZ, MARTIN GUGGENHEIM & ANTHONY G. AMSTERDAM, NAT'L JUV. DEFENDER CTR., TRIAL MANUAL FOR DEFENSE ATTORNEYS IN JUVENILE DELINQUENCY CASES 239 (2012).

## Box 3: Motions Practice

Counsel in juvenile delinquency cases should consider filing the following motions:

1. Motions for discovery:
   a. Motion for a Bill of Particulars
   b. Motion for a List of Prosecution Witnesses
   c. Motions Requesting Production and/or Inspection of
      i. Physical objects

*Continued*

**31**

## Box 3: Motions Practice *Continued*

ii. Medical and scientific reports

iii. Police and other investigative reports

iv. Written and oral statements of the respondent

v. Written and oral statements of any co-respondents, adult co-perpetrators, or other alleged accomplices

vi. Statements of witnesses

vii. Official records (maintained by detention facilities, prisons, jails, hospitals, probation departments, and so forth) relating to the respondent, co-respondents, adult co-perpetrators, and prosecution and defense witnesses

viii. Criminal records of the respondent, co-respondents, adult co-perpetrators, and prosecution and defense witnesses

ix. Grand jury transcripts, if grand jury proceedings were held in connection with any co-perpetrators charged as adults

x. Photographs and other visual aids shown to witnesses by investigating officers for purposes of identification

2. Motions to suppress tangible evidence, confessions and incriminating statements, and identification testimony

3. Motions for severance of counts or respondents:

a. Motions to dismiss the charging paper for failure to allege facts justifying the joinder of counts

b. Motions challenging misjoinder of charge

c. Motions for a severance of charges on the ground of prejudicial joinder

d. Motions challenging misjoinder of respondents

e. Motions for a severance of respondents on the ground of prejudicial joinder

    i. Severance on the Basis of a Co-respondent's Confession Implicating the Respondent

    ii. Severance on the Basis of the Respondent's Need to Call the Co-respondent as a Witness

    iii. Severance on the Basis of the Respondents' Conflicting

and Irreconcilable Defenses

    iv.   Severance on the Basis of the Disparity of the Evidence against the Respondents

4.   Motions challenging the sufficiency of the petition or the jurisdiction of the court:

    a.   Failure of the Charging Paper to Allege Facts Constituting a Crime

        i.   Failure to Charge Acts That Are Criminal in Nature

        ii.   Failure to Allege Facts That Make Out Every Element of the Charged Offense

        iii.   Lack of Specificity

    b.   Jurisdictional Defects: Maximum Age And Minimum Age Requirements for Juvenile Court Prosecution

    c.   Dismissal of the Charging Paper for Failure to Establish Venue

    d.   Technical Defects in the Charging Paper

    e.   Statute of Limitations

    f.   Double Jeopardy

5.   Motions seeking a change of venue or recusal of the judge

6.   Motions to dismiss for social reasons

*Adapted from* Randy Hertz, Martin Guggenheim & Anthony G. Amsterdam, Nat'l Juv. Defender Ctr., Trial Manual for Defense Attorneys in Juvenile Delinquency Cases 153-54, 203-06, 366-68, 382-90 (2012).

# CHAPTER THREE

## Finding a New Home
# Representing Children in Immigration Actions

By Gail Chang Bohr, Fue Lo Thao
and Maisue Xiong

### PART I: ENIYE'S STORY

When Eniye told her seventh-grade classmate that her uncle had caused the bruise on her cheek, she had no idea that she would be removed from the uncle's home as a child in need of protection or services, a CHIPS child, and placed in a shelter. Only a short few months before, Eniye had come to America, accompanying a man she called "Uncle" and his wife and their children. Back in her native Nigeria, she had been the servant girl to the family and basically had grown up with this family. Eniye remembered nothing about her parents—she did not know who they were or from what village they came. She only knew that she was about five years old when she was brought to the city to live with the uncle and his family. She cooked and cleaned for them. She did not attend school in Nigeria. She did not know her real age or even her full name.

Fue Lo Thao, Esq. is Special Assistant County Attorney, Ramsey County Attorney's Office. Maisue Xiong, Esq. is Law Clerk to the Honorable Gail Chang Bohr, Judge, Second Judicial District of Minnesota. The section on Special Immigrant Juvenile Status was written by Rebecca Scholtz, Esq., Liman Fellow, Immigration Law Project, Mid-Minnesota Legal Aid.

Eniye and the family with whom she lived belonged to a minority group, the Ogoni, or "Rivers," people, who were persecuted by the Nigerian government. A Christian group sponsored the uncle and his family to come to America as refugees and helped them settle in St. Paul, Minnesota; Eniye came as part of the family. The Christian group made sure all the children were enrolled in school, so at the age of 14 or 15, Eniye attended school for the first time. But she was still expected to cook and clean for the family while trying to do her homework and participating in school activities. One day she returned home from a school activity too late to get the cooking and cleaning done. Her uncle struck her in the face and left marks. Although this was not the first time it had happened, Eniye had not told anyone about the physical abuse. The next day at school, one of her classmates saw the bruise and asked Eniye about it. The classmate insisted that Eniye tell a teacher. The teacher in turn called County Child Protection Services.

Eniye was removed from the uncle's home and taken to a shelter placement, where she stayed while Child Protection investigated and figured out where she should go. The Christian group that had sponsored the family became involved in the situation. The uncle now had a criminal offense on his record, which could affect his ability to remain in the United States.

The family decided together with the Christian group that they should send Eniye back to Nigeria, because they thought she was only going to cause more trouble for the man and his family if she remained in the United States. Child Protection was still investigating the case and agreed to that plan because as long as Eniye was not with the uncle, the abuser, they did not have to provide services to Eniye. The uncle gave Child Protection a phone number in Nigeria that he said belonged to Eniye's parents. The agency social worker called the number in Nigeria and spoke with someone who agreed to take Eniye. This group presented the plan to the juvenile court judge, who approved it without having all the information. Child Protection instructed the uncle to buy a plane ticket for Eniye to return to Nigeria.

With six days left before Eniye was to be placed on the plane, the County Attorney's Office called Children's Law Center of Minnesota (CLC) about Eniye. CLC provides legal representation on a pro bono basis to children in foster care. CLC is appointed by the court or children contact CLC directly for a lawyer. In Eniye's case, because the county had decided to send her back

**36**

to Nigeria, CLC did not receive the appointment. Nevertheless, the County Attorney's Office called CLC on a Friday to see if CLC was in agreement with the plan for Eniye to return to Nigeria. A CLC attorney immediately arranged to meet with the child that weekend in the shelter placement.

Eniye was of slight build and looked younger than the given age of 14. Eniye spoke English (Nigeria had been a British colony). Eniye was nervous and was physically shaking when the CLC attorney met with her. She made it clear that she was very frightened at the prospect of being sent back to Nigeria because she did not know where she was going or with whom she was going to live. She had been sent to live with the uncle as a very young child, in her estimation about age five. She had never visited the family village or even had contact with the people in Nigeria contacted by Child Protection—the people who now claimed they were her parents. She did not know the names of her parents nor where they lived, so she had no way of knowing if they were telling the truth.

The CLC attorney immediately researched the conditions in Nigeria and in particular the "Rivers" people—the Ogoni. They were a persecuted people. One of their own—Ken Saro-Wiwa, a poet and activist who was framed for murder—was publicly executed by the government. The CLC attorney realized that Eniye was in the United States as a refugee. The attorney also sought out country experts including an attorney she knew who was from a different part of Nigeria. This individual explained that in Nigeria, "Uncle" was an honorific title not having anything to do with blood relationship and that it was not unusual for parents to place their daughters at a young age in families to be the servant girl.

The CLC attorney was concerned about Eniye's safety on several grounds. As a refugee, she would be subject to persecution by the government if she returned to Nigeria. In addition, Child Protection had not conducted an adequate investigation to determine if the people purporting to be her parents were indeed her parents or even whether they were suitable caretakers. If indeed they were her parents, these people had given Eniye to the uncle to be a servant girl; and if they were not her parents, there was no way to know if she would be safe with them.

The CLC attorney had two choices. She could either remove the case to federal court since only the U.S. government has jurisdiction over deportation, and the juvenile court essentially had ordered a deportation. Or she could bring a Child in Need of Protection or Services (CHIPS) Petition before the same judge in juvenile court, and request that the judge vacate his order permitting the child to be sent back to Nigeria and instead grant the child's motion for a CHIPS Petition. The attorney had only two business days before the child was to leave the country.

In her conversations with Eniye, the attorney had found out that she wanted to remain in the United States because she knew no one in Nigeria. Eniye had made it abundantly clear she was afraid of being sent back to Nigeria. Thus, the attorney decided to bring a CHIPS petition. If the juvenile court judge denied the petition, she could still pursue an injunction in federal court.

The attorney filed an emergency CHIPS petition requesting that the judge vacate his prior order and instead declare Eniye to be a child in need of protection or services. The judge agreed to hold an evidentiary hearing on the petition. At the evidentiary hearing, the social worker was a witness for the county. She explained that the uncle had given her the phone number; she said she had talked to the parents who had agreed to take Eniye.

Upon cross-examination by the CLC attorney, the social worker admitted that she could not verify that the people she had spoken to were in fact Eniye's parents. She had no copy of a birth certificate. She did not know the names of the parents or the names of the people with whom she had spoken on the telephone. She had taken the phone number from the uncle as given and relied on his word alone that the people on the other end of the line were Eniye's parents. She also admitted that she had not talked with anyone in the U.S. State Department about country conditions or the status of the Ogoni people in Nigeria.

With her petition, the CLC attorney included a memorandum outlining the country conditions for the Ogoni people in Nigeria and explaining to the juvenile court judge that Eniye had entered the United States as a refugee, as she belonged to a group of people who had been persecuted in her home country. Consequently, the attorney argued that only the U.S. federal government had jurisdiction over whether Eniye could be sent back to Nigeria, something that neither Child Protection nor the Christian group had taken into consideration before developing the plan to put her on a plane and send her back to strangers. After the evidentiary hearing, the juvenile court judge vacated his original order giving permission to the county to send Eniye back to Nigeria and instead granted Eniye's Child in Need of Protection or Services Petition. Eniye was placed with a foster parent in St. Paul, and continued to go to school. She is now a permanent U.S. resident, having applied for a green card based on her legal immigration status as a refugee.

## PART II: REPRESENTING UNACCOMPANIED ALIEN CHILDREN
### Overview

Eniye's story demonstrates the precarious situation of children without legal status who are in the United States without family. Many unaccompanied alien children are in a unique situation in which they have little control over the circumstances of their entry into the United States.[1] They are extremely vulnerable because they have no knowledge about the immigration laws or options for seeking legal relief.[2] Unaccompanied alien children (UAC) are children under the age of 18 who leave their home country to embark on a perilous journey to the United States on their own.[3] Unaccompanied minors who make the journey from their home countries to come to the United States do so for a number of reasons. They may come to rejoin families already in the United States, to find work to support families in their home country, or to escape abusive homes or even persecution in their home countries.[4] This group of children is especially vulnerable to becoming prey to exploitation, abuse, and human trafficking because of their young age, their lack of lawful immigration status, the absence of parents or legal

---

1. Deborah Lee et al., Immigrant Legal Res. Ctr., Update on Legal Relief Options for Unaccompanied Alien Children Following the Enactment of the William Wilberforce Trafficking Victims Protection Reauthorization Act of 2008 7 (2009), *available at* http://www.ilrc.org/files/235_tvpra_practice_advisory.infonet.pdf.
2. *Id.*
3. *About Unaccompanied Children's Services*, Office of Refugee Resettlement, http://www.acf.hhs.gov/programs/orr/programs/ucs/about (last visited June 13, 2013).
4. *Id.*

guardians to provide care and custody, and the complex laws and policies that govern the United States's legal and immigration systems.

It is impossible to know how many unaccompanied alien children are actually present in the United States. However, the United States Department of Homeland Security (DHS) and the Office of Refugee Resettlement (ORR) maintain data after an unaccompanied child has been apprehended. (The data does not include unaccompanied children who are living in the United States illegally and have not been apprehended.) Up to 15% of unaccompanied alien children enter the U.S. immigration system as a result of being apprehended by local, state, or federal officials.[5] They are often detected as they try to enter the United States at a port of entry or through worksite enforcement actions, operations to combat smuggling and human trafficking, or their involvement in the juvenile or criminal justice systems.[6] When an unaccompanied child is taken into DHS custody and placed at a temporary DHS detention facility, the child is interviewed. If it is determined that the child does not have a parent or legal guardian within geographical proximity and the child is younger than 18 years old, a referral is made to ORR.[7] ORR assumes custody of the child and is responsible for the care and placement of the child.[8] DHS commences immigration proceedings to remove the child from the United States and to return the child to his/her home country, while ORR provides services for the child, which can include foster care, education, health care, mental health services, case management, and vocational training.[9] Most unaccompanied alien children remain in ORR custody from one week to four months.[10] (See Box 1, "General Statistics of UAC in Care in Fiscal Year 2013.")

---

5. Olga Byrne & Elise Miller, Vera Institute of Justice, The Flow of Unaccompanied Children Through the Immigration System: A Resource for Practitioners, Policy Makers and Researchers 4 (2012), *available at* http://www.vera.org/sites/default/files/resources/downloads/the-flow-of-unaccompanied-children-through-the-immigration-system.pdf.
6. *Id.* at 8–10.
7. *Id.* at 10.
8. *Id.*
9. *Id.* at 14.
10. *Id.* at 4.

## Box 1

### General Statistics of UAC in Care in Fiscal Year 2013
- Total number of UAC referred: 24,668
- 73% males
- 27% females
- 24% are below the age of 14

### Most Common Native Countries of UAC in Fiscal Year 2013
- Guatemala (37%)
- El Salvador (26%)
- Honduras (30%)
- Mexico (3%)
- Ecuador (2%)
- Other (3%)

In fiscal year 2012, the UAC program had an unprecented increase in referrals from DHS. The program's size doubled over the previous eight years, which had averaged 6,775 referrals per year. The increase continued in fiscal year 2013.

*Source: About Unaccompanied Children's Services*, OFFICE OF REFUGEE RESETTLEMENT, http://www.acf.hhs.gov/programs/orr/programs/ucs /about (last visited February 14, 2014).

All unaccompanied alien children face difficulties in the U.S. immigration system. The Sixth Amendment to the United States Constitution does not guarantee unaccompanied alien children the right to counsel. Rather, children must rely on pro bono attorneys or other volunteers to navigate a complex immigration system. Additionally, children who seek nonimmigrant visa status, such as the T visa or the U visa (see below), may be held in detention and continuously face the threat of deportation.[11] Children often arrive in the United States with debt and are generally in poverty without access to general public welfare benefits.[12] Unaccompanied alien children who qualify for nonimmigrant visa status are often victims of trafficking or crimes that significantly affect their physical and mental well-being.

Helping an unaccompanied alien child through the process of obtaining lawful residence in the United States has a certain level of finality, but the damage that is caused by the crimes against these children may take a lifetime to mend. Attorneys play a crucial role in assisting unaccompanied minor children in obtaining status in the United States as the first step in providing these children with safety, stability, and hope for the future.

## Legal Tools to Assist Unaccompanied Alien Minors

Approximately 40% of children admitted to ORR custody are eligible for a form of legal relief from removal proceedings because they are victims of crime or trafficking, are eligible for asylum, or are eligible for special immigrant juvenile status.[13] In 2010, there were 7,020 children in ORR custody. Of those children, 2,830 children were eligible for some type of potential relief from removal.[14] Some children were eligible for more than one type of relief.

Eniye was granted legal immigration status as a refugee when she came to the United States with the "uncle" and his family. As described in more detail below, there are a variety of legal statuses that attorneys may seek for unaccompanied alien minors. If Eniye had not already had legal status, she would have been eligible to apply for a number of the statuses listed below in Box 2.

---

11. ANGIE JUNCK ET AL., IMMIGRANT LEGAL RES. CTR., SPECIAL IMMIGRANT JUVENILE STATUS AND OTHER IMMIGRATION OPTIONS FOR CHILDREN AND YOUTH 1-2 (Jan. 2010), *available at* http://www.ilrc.org/files/sijs-2010-toc.pdf.
12. *Id.* at 1-1, 1-2.
13. BYRNE & MILLER, *supra* note 5, at 4.
14. *Id.* at 25.

## Box 2

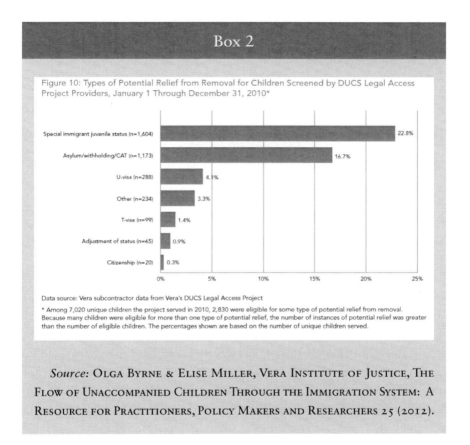

Figure 10: Types of Potential Relief from Removal for Children Screened by DUCS Legal Access Project Providers, January 1 Through December 31, 2010*

Data source: Vera subcontractor data from Vera's DUCS Legal Access Project

\* Among 7,020 unique children the project served in 2010, 2,830 were eligible for some type of potential relief from removal. Because many children were eligible for more than one type of potential relief, the number of instances of potential relief was greater than the number of eligible children. The percentages shown are based on the number of unique children served.

*Source:* OLGA BYRNE & ELISE MILLER, VERA INSTITUTE OF JUSTICE, THE FLOW OF UNACCOMPANIED CHILDREN THROUGH THE IMMIGRATION SYSTEM: A RESOURCE FOR PRACTITIONERS, POLICY MAKERS AND RESEARCHERS 25 (2012).

## Human Trafficking Victims and T Visas

Victims of trafficking come in all forms, sizes, and mental conditions. Human traffickers prey on vulnerable individuals, children, and young women. Typically, human traffickers will trick their prey using promises of wealth, applying coercion, or gaining the confidence of the child. Others may forcefully kidnap the child.[15] U.S. government–sponsored research completed in 2006 estimates that approximately 800,000 people are trafficked

---

15. TYLER MARIE CHRISTENSEN, UN HIGH COMM'R FOR REFUGEES, TRAFFICKING FOR SEXUAL EXPLOITATION: VICTIM PROTECTION IN INTERNATIONAL AND DOMESTIC ASYLUM LAW 1–2 (Apr. 2011), *available at* http://www.unhcr-centraleurope.org/pdf/resources/

across national borders every year, which does not include the millions who are trafficked within their own countries.[16] Approximately 80% of transnational victims are women and girls, and up to 50% are minors. The majority of transnational victims are females trafficked into commercial sexual exploitation.[17]

Often unaccompanied alien children are abandoned or neglected by their biological parents. They are brought to this country by a stranger or "friend of the family" whom they refer to with an honorific term because of tradition, such as the uncle in Eniye's case.[18] Having no one to turn to, these children face significant societal difficulties. They are typically aware that they are in the United States illegally and thus are afraid to seek help from any organizations designed to help them. Moreover, Americans may see these children as perpetrators rather than victims, creating an additional barrier to a child seeking to break free from his/her trafficker.[19]

Unaccompanied alien children are dependent upon the human trafficker who brought them here to provide food, shelter, and clothing. Victims often are poor, unemployed, or underemployed and are enticed by promises of wealth from the human trafficker. Additionally, these children typically have had little or no schooling and may not speak English.[20]

The Victims of Trafficking and Violence Protection Act of 2000,[21] the Trafficking Victims Protection Reauthorization Act of 2005,[22] and the William Wilberforce Trafficking Victims Protection Reauthorization Act of 2008 (TVPRA) provide key tools to trafficking victims and their advocates.[23]

---

evaluation-and-research/trafficking-for-sexual-exploitation-victim-protection-in-internationa l-and-domestic-asylum-law-tyler-marie-christensen.html.

16. U.S. DEP'T OF STATE, TRAFFICKING IN PERSONS REPORT 8 (June 2007), *available at* http://www.state.gov/documents/organization/82902.pdf.

17. *Id.*

18. JUNCK, *supra* note 11, at 1-1.

19. *Id.*

20. *Id.*

21. Victims of Trafficking and Violence Protection Act of 2000, Pub. L. No. 106-386, 114 Stat. 1464 (2000).

22. Trafficking Victims Protection Reauthorization Act of 2005, Pub. L. No. 109-164, 119 Stat. 3558 (2006).

23. William Wilberforce Trafficking Victims Protection Reauthorization Act of 2008, Pub. L. No. 110-457, 122 Stat. 5044 (2008). The TVPRA was also included in its entirety as an

TVPRA and its subsequent amendments extended protections and visa status—including the T visa and U visa—to victims of severe forms of human trafficking and of other crimes who assist law enforcement in the investigation and prosecution of trafficking criminals.[24]

---

**Practice Tip**: A child may be eligible for more than one type of immigration benefit. Be sure to check the requirements for all immigration benefits before filing.

---

An unaccompanied alien child may apply for nonimmigrant status if he/she is a victim of severe forms of trafficking and assists law enforcement in the investigation and prosecution of human trafficking cases.[25] Specifically, all trafficking victims, including minors, may apply for a T visa.[26] According to the United States Citizenship and Immigration Services (USCIS), an average of 800 victims and their families have applied for T visas each year since 2002. An average of 560 are accepted each year. More recently, in 2012, there were more than 1,680 applications for T visas, and 1,432 of those applications were approved (674 were for victims and the remainder for their families).[27] The granting of T visas was capped at 5,000 because at the time of the inception of the visas, Congress feared that they would cause a surge of fraud. The number of applications for T visas is increasing

---

amendment to the Violence Against Women Reauthorization Act of 2013. *See* Pub. L. No. 113-4, 127 Stat. 54 (2013); Violence Against Women Reauthorization Act, S. 47, 113th Cong. (2013).

24. LEE, *supra* note 1, at 1.

25. Immigration and Naturalization Act § 101(a)(15)(T), 8 U.S.C. § 1101(a)(15)(T) (2013).

26. Victims of Trafficking and Violence Protection Act of 2000, Pub. L. No. 106-386, 114 Stat. 1464 (2000).

27. U.S. CITIZENSHIP & IMMIGR. SERV., Form I-914—Application for T Nonimmigrant Status and Form I-918—Petition for U Nonimmigrant Status: Service-Wide Receipts, Approvals, and Denials; Fiscal Years: 2002 through 2013 (October 2012), *available at* http://www.uscis.gov/USCIS/Resources/Reports%20and%20Studies/Immigration%20Forms%20Data/Victims/I914T-I918U-visastatistics-2013-Oct.csv.

every year but has remained less than one-half of the maximum allotment of 5,000.[28]

To qualify for the T visa, a person must (1) be a victim of a severe form of trafficking in persons, as defined in section 103 of the Victims of Trafficking and Violence Protection Act of 2000; (2) be physically present in the United States on account of the trafficking; (3) comply with any reasonable requests for assistance in the investigation or prosecution (or be under the age of 18); and (4) suffer extreme hardship involving unusual and severe harm if removed from the United States.[29] The TVPRA defines "severe forms of trafficking in persons" as (a) sex trafficking in which a commercial sex act is induced by force, fraud, or coercion, or in which the person induced to perform such an act has not attained 18 years of age; or (b) the recruitment, harboring, transportation, provision, or obtaining of a person for labor or services, through the use of force, fraud, or coercion for the purpose of subjection to involuntary servitude, peonage, debt bondage, or slavery. A victim need not be physically transported from one location to another in order for the crime to fall within these definitions.[30] A useful resource for researching child trafficking trends is the tier evaluation conducted by the U.S. Department of State as a result of the TVPRA.[31] Through this tier evaluation, countries are evaluated on their compliance with trafficking standards throughout the globe and placed on a three-tier scale in order of the severity of trafficking violations.

---

**Practice Tip:** To assist you in discovering countries with high levels of trafficking, refer to the U.S. Department of State Tier Reports, which provide the public an annual analysis of what countries are complying with minimal standards to prevent human trafficking.[32]

---

28. U.S. DEP'T OF STATE, TRAFFICKING IN PERSONS REPORT 15 (June 2012), *available at* http://www.state.gov/documents/organization/192587.pdf.

29. Victims of Trafficking and Violence Protection Act of 2000, Pub. L. No. 106-386, 114 Stat. 1464 (2000).

30. 22 U.S.C. § 7102(9) (2011).

31. U.S. Dep't of State, *Trafficking in Persons Report*, available at http://www.state.gov /j/tip/rls/tiprpt/. The Report is published annually.

32. *Id.*

## Crime Victims and U Visas

Victims of any age are eligible for the U Nonimmigrant Status, also known as the "U visa," if they have been a victim of certain qualifying criminal activity that violates any federal, state, or local criminal law and they have suffered substantial physical or mental abuse as a result of a crime.[33] Specifically, the U visa requires that the Secretary of Homeland Security determine that, with respect to certain "qualifying criminal activities"[34] that occurred in the United States, the alien suffered substantial physical or mental abuse and the alien (or in the case of an alien child under the age of 16, the parent, guardian, or next friend of the alien) possesses information concerning the criminal activity and has been helpful, is being helpful, or is likely to be helpful to authorities investigating or prosecuting the crimes.[35]

The eligibility criteria for U visas is broader than that for T visas; accordingly, a significantly higher number of applications are submitted for U visas. According to the USCIS, 24,768 U visa applications (including adult applications) were submitted by victims in 2012, and 10,122 were approved.[36] Congress created a cap of 10,000 U visas per fiscal year (October 1 through September 30);[37] the cap has been reached every year since 2010.[38]

## The Violence Against Women Act (VAWA)

The Violence Against Women Act (VAWA) in the Immigration and Nationality Act allows spouses, children, and parents of U.S. citizens and lawful permanent residents to petition for legal status without having to rely

---

33. Immigration and Naturalization Act § 101(a)(15)(U), 8 U.S.C. § 1101(a)(15)(U) (2013).

34. Qualifying criminal activities include abduction, abusive sexual contact, blackmail, domestic violence, extortion, false imprisonment, female genital mutilation, felonious assault, hostage, incest, involuntary servitude, kidnapping, manslaughter, murder, obstruction of justice, peonage, perjury, prostitution, rape, sexual assault, sexual exploitation, slave trade, torture, trafficking, witness tampering, unlawful criminal restraint, and attempt, conspiracy, or solicitation to commit any of these crimes. 8 U.S.C. § 1101(a)(15)(U)(iii).

35. Id.

36. U.S. CITIZENSHIP & IMMIGR. SERV., *supra* note 27.

37. *USCIS Reaches Milestone for Third Straight Year: 10,000 U Visas Approved in Fiscal Year 2012*, U.S. CITIZENSHIP & IMMIG. SERV., http://www.uscis.gov/portal/site/uscis/menuitem.5af9bb95919f35e66f614176543f6d1a/?vgnextoid=5cd8f03530a49310VgnVCM100000082ca60aRCRD&vgnextchannel=68439c7755cb9010VgnVCM10000045f3d6a1RCRD. *See also* U.S. CITIZENSHIP & IMMIGR. SERV., *supra* note 27.

38. Id.

on their abuser's sponsorship.[39] An unmarried child under age 21 may self-petition to gain legal immigration status if the minor is a child of a U.S. citizen or permanent resident; the child is a victim of abuse from that parent; the abuse occurred in the United States; the child resided with the abusive parent; the child has evidence to prove his/her relationship to the parent; and the child, if over the age of 14, can provide evidence that he or she has good moral character.[40]

Proving a case of VAWA can be difficult for an unaccompanied alien child because VAWA requires that a child have a parent or legal guardian who is a lawful permanent resident of the United States or is a U.S. citizen. A child's ability to utilize VAWA to gain legal immigrant status is dependent upon his or her familial relationship with the parent who already has legal status in the United States.

## Asylum

Eniye came to the United States as a refugee. She was forced to flee her country because of persecution of her social group, the "Rivers," or Ogoni, people in Nigeria. If Eniye had not had legal status as a refugee and had been in the United States without legal status, she could have applied for asylum.

Asylum is a form of protection for individuals who are at risk of removal from the United States to be returned to their home country. Asylum protects individuals who have been persecuted or who have a well-founded fear of persecution on account of their (1) race, (2) religion, (3) nationality, (4) membership in a particular social group, or (5)political opinion.[41] The asylum process is available to people who are already physically present in the United States. A person may apply for asylum regardless of his/her immigration status and whether he/she is in the United States legally or

---

39. *Battered Spouse, Children, & Parents*, U.S. CITIZENSHIP & IMMIG. SERV., http://www .uscis.gov/humanitarian/battered-spouse-children-parents (last visited June 13, 2013).

40. *Id.*

41. U.S. CITIZENSHIP & IMMIGR. SERV., OVERVIEW OF THE ASYLUM PROCESS, http://www .uscis.gov/USCIS/Humanitarian/Refugees%20&%20Asylum/Asylum/Information%20Guides %20For%20Prospective%20Applicants/info-guide-for-prospective-asylum-applicants-english .pdf (last visited June 12, 2013).

illegally.[42] The applicant may petition for asylum within one year of his/her arrival in the United States.[43] But the INA § 208 has been amended to specifically exempt unaccompanied alien children from the one-year deadline for applying for asylum.[44] Unaccompanied alien children under 18 years old who have no parent or legal guardian in the United States available to provide care and physical custody may apply for asylum.

Asylum interviews are to be conducted in a nonadversarial way, and the TVPRA states that the child's developmental needs should be taken into consideration along with the asylum application.[45] But proving a valid asylum case still is difficult for unaccompanied alien children. In many asylum cases, children's ability to claim asylum is derivative of their parents' asylum claims. Unaccompanied alien children must prove either that they have been persecuted in the past or that they have a well-founded fear of being persecuted in the future based on one of the five grounds enumerated in the preceding paragraph.[46]

In asylum cases, especially human trafficking cases, victims may have difficulty producing documentary evidence because of the lack of valid identity documents, embarrassment about the sexual and physical violence the victim has endured, the fear of retaliation by traffickers against the victim and her/his family, and the trauma she/he has experienced.[47] The Board of Immigration Appeals (BIA) has stated "threats to life, confinement, torture, and economic restrictions so severe that they constitute a threat to life or freedom" will amount to persecution.[48] The United Nations High Commissioner on Refugees Handbook also explains that the alleged acts should be examined to determine if they can reasonably justify a claim of

---

42. *Asylum*, U.S. CITIZENSHIP & IMMIG. SERV., http://www.uscis.gov/portal/site/uscis/menuitem.5af9bb95919f35e66f614176543f6d1a/?vgnextoid=c1d80efdea7fe010VgnVCM1000000ecd190aRCRD&vgnextchannel=f39d3e4d77d73210VgnVCM100000082ca60aRCRD (last visited June 12, 2013).

43. *Id.*

44. LEE, *supra* note 1, at 7.

45. *Id.* at 7–8.

46. CHRISTENSEN, *supra* note 15, at 8.

47. *See id.* at 7.

48. *Id.* at 6.

a well-founded fear of persecution.[49]

It is important that attorneys and practitioners refer to the United Nations High Commissioner on Refugees to discover background information about countries that have significant issues with persecution and violence.[50] Specific countries' reports are completed annually that outline the human rights issues prevalent in various countries. These country reports may help establish proof of persecution that warrants a well-founded fear.

## Special Immigrant Juvenile Status

A largely underutilized provision in the federal immigration law known as Special Immigrant Juvenile Status (SIJS) allows certain undocumented children in the state juvenile court system to acquire lawful permanent resident (LPR) status in a relatively short time frame.[51] Accessing LPR status through SIJS confers many benefits on vulnerable immigrant children, including protection from deportation, obtaining work authorization and a social security number, eligibility for some public benefits, and access to financial aid for college.

Specifically, federal law requires state court findings before a child can seek SIJS from the U.S. Citizenship and Immigration Services. The required findings are that (1) it is not in the child's best interest to be returned to the country of origin; (2) the child's reunification with one or both parents is not viable due to abuse, neglect, or abandonment, or a similar basis under state law; and (3) the child has been declared dependent on the court or legally committed to, or placed by the court under the custody of a state agency or department or individual or entity appointed by the court.[52] These findings

---

49. *Id.*
50. UN HIGH COMM'R ON REFUGEES, http://www.unhcr.org/cgi-bin/texis/vtx/home (last visited June 12, 2013). The full title of the Handbook is, United Nations High Commissioner on Refugees, Handbook on Procedures and Criteria for Determining Refugee Status Under the 1951 Convention and the 1967 Protocol Relating to the Status of Refugees, UN Doc. HCR/IP/4/Eng/Rev.1 (2nd ed. 1992), para. 53, *available at* http://www.unhcr.org/3d58e13b4.html.
51. *See* 8 U.S.C. § 1101(a)(27)(J). While the SIJS statute was originally enacted in 1990, important amendments were made in 2008 through the Trafficking Victims Protection Reauthorization Act (TVPRA), Pub. L. No. 110-457, 122 Stat. 5044 (TVPRA) (2008). The TVPRA amendments substantially broadened the class of children eligible for SIJS.
52. *See* 8 U.S.C. § 1101(a)(27)(J).

can be obtained in any number of state court proceedings that deal with children, including dependency, delinquency, adoption, custody, and guardianship.[53] The child must be under 21 and unmarried to qualify for SIJS.[54] Once the predicate state court order has been obtained, the child can apply for SIJS (a process that involves several steps) with the help of an experienced immigration practitioner.[55]

Anecdotal evidence suggests that many children go through the juvenile court system without being identified as SIJS eligible and thus lose out on this extremely valuable benefit. Eligible youth lose the opportunity to apply for SIJS when they turn 21. They may also lose the opportunity if court jurisdiction terminates before the SIJS application is filed or, in some cases, adjudicated. Best practice is to identify potentially eligible children at an early stage in the juvenile court proceeding and consult with an experienced immigration attorney who may further assess SIJS eligibility and, if the child is eligible, assist him or her in obtaining SIJS.

---

53. While the statute provides that SIJS findings are to be made in a "juvenile court," that term is defined broadly to include any court with authority to make decisions about the custody and care of juveniles. *See* 8 C.F.R. § 204.11 (2009).

54. *See* 8 C.F.R.. § 204.11 (2009).

55. The child must remain unmarried through the SIJS process. However, if the child exceeds the age of 21 after the application has been filed, the application cannot be denied on that basis. Similarly, if court jurisdiction terminates after the application has been filed based on the child's age, the SIJS application cannot be denied on that basis.

# CHAPTER FOUR

## Staying on Track
# Protecting Youth in School Discipline Actions

By Brent Pattison

### PART I: JOHN'S STORY

A young man's embarrassment about his slow reading resulted in his expulsion from school. Fortunately, a lawyer was able to get the school district not only to reinstate him but also to evaluate him so that he could get the special education services he needed.

Fourteen-year-old John, a Native American youth from the Seattle area, was already struggling in school when the incident happened. He had a long disciplinary history at school, mostly for minor disobedience or disrespect, and a lot of absences. Although it was the middle of John's sophomore year, he had not earned a single high school credit and was failing all his classes.

Then one day, his language arts teacher asked John to read aloud in class; John refused. When the teacher pressed him to read, John used some colorful language and tried to leave the classroom. The teacher asked John to go back to his seat, and blocked the door. John tried to run past the teacher, bumped into him, and took off down the hallway, yelling, "You are lucky I'm not a bad kid. If I was a bad kid I'd kick your ass." The teacher called the principal, who called the school resource officer. John was arrested for harassment and assault and brought to juvenile detention.

John was arraigned on charges two weeks later in juvenile court. When his public defender realized he had been expelled for the same incident, he referred John to TeamChild, a civil legal aid program for youth in Seattle. An attorney from TeamChild contacted John regarding the expulsion; his parents said they had received no paperwork from the school district but the principal had told them John was expelled. The TeamChild attorney advised John he could appeal the expulsion, and helped John write a letter requesting an appeal.

At first, school district officials claimed John was not entitled to a hearing because he had failed to request it within three days of the incident. But John's lawyer pushed back, arguing that the district's failure to provide legally required written notice about the discipline and his appeal rights excused the delay. The school district reluctantly scheduled a hearing.

In the letter requesting a hearing, John's attorney also requested all of John's school and disciplinary records. The attorney learned that although John had been evaluated for special educational needs in middle school, the high school had failed to do any evaluations. His parents had previously asked the school district to evaluate whether John needed special education. But the school district's position was that John was not attending consistently enough to rule out that his academic problems were really just a function of poor attendance. The middle school evaluation showed that John's IQ was in the borderline range of eligibility for special education services, but he narrowly missed being eligible. The evaluation also noted that his expressive and receptive language skills were very low.

The lawyer's interviews with John and his parents revealed other illuminating information. They said John was incredibly frustrated at school. His reading skills were limited, and all of his classes, even science and math, now required a heavy dose of textbook reading. John frequently felt confused and lost at school, and often slipped out of school at lunch time and skipped his afternoon classes. John told his attorney that the reason he was so upset on the day of the incident was that he was nervous about reading aloud. John was adamant that he never meant to threaten the teacher—he was just upset and trying to explain he was not a bad kid.

At the hearing, the school district lawyer explained that the district had a "zero tolerance" policy regarding threats, and that John had made inappropriate, unwanted physical contact with the teacher. The school district presented no witnesses. Instead, it just offered the hearing officer a thick stack of documents relating to the incident and all John's prior disciplinary and attendance records. John's lawyer objected to the fact that all of the evidence was hearsay. Students in Washington State have a right to question and cross-examine witnesses, and it was not possible to do that when the only evidence was in written statements. The hearing officer agreed and required the district to present testimony from John's teacher. Subsequently, the teacher explained what had happened, but also acknowledged that he had not really felt threatened by John, who just seemed like a frustrated, struggling student, and not a delinquent. The teacher also acknowledged that when he saw how upset John was, he wished, in hindsight, that he had not put himself between John and the door. He should have just let John step outside to cool off. John's lawyer asked the teacher if he had ever seen John's middle school special education evaluation and what it said about John's reading level. The teacher had never reviewed the evaluation.

John's lawyer then presented testimony from John's mother about how hard school had been for John, his generally good behavior at home, and all of John's activities with his tribe. She explained that John had never assaulted anyone before, and his only behavioral challenges had occurred at school. She talked about all of their efforts to get John help with his reading and said that she hoped that good could come from this if the school would focus attention on his academic problems.

John's lawyer did not want John to testify, given the pending charges in juvenile court, but asked for permission for John to make a brief statement. John explained his frustration at school, that he needed help in reading, and that he wanted to make something of his life and he could not do that without an education. He had never meant to threaten or hurt his teacher.

In closing, the school district lawyer emphasized the district's zero tolerance policy for threats, arguing that the evidence might support John requesting readmission next semester but did not support overturning the current expulsion. John's lawyer argued that under the district's own policy regarding threats, John's behavior was not a threat as it would not have made a reasonable person feel any fear, and the teacher had said he was never fearful. John's lawyer submitted a threat assessment guide developed

**55**

for schools by the FBI, and noted that under the FBI protocol, the alleged threat was not a serious one because it was vague, conditional, made as John was leaving the classroom, and from a student with no previous history of threatening behavior. To justify the most serious form of disciplinary exclusion, the school had to show that the nature and circumstances of the incident warranted expulsion. Given John's borderline IQ, reading problems, and problems with expressive language, the evidence showed that John had not meant to threaten or harm the teacher in any way. Instead, the lawyer argued that John should be immediately reinstated and a new special education evaluation should be initiated.

The hearing officer ruled in John's favor the next day, ordering his reinstatement and suggesting, but not requiring, a new evaluation. John's lawyer faxed a copy of the hearing officer's findings of fact and conclusions of law to John's public defender. John's defense attorney used the decision to get the prosecutor to divert the charges from juvenile court, and John avoided further contact with the court by doing some volunteer work at school.

The school district ultimately agreed to reevaluate John for special education, and his second evaluation determined he was eligible for special education services. He remained in most of his classes, but he received extra support with reading, and his assignments in his regular classes were adapted in light of his challenges. John was offered a peer note-taker and the opportunity to listen to audio recordings from his textbooks. He finished the rest of the year with no disciplinary incidents.

## PART II: ADVOCATING FOR YOUTH IN SCHOOL DISCIPLINE MATTERS

The use of disciplinary exclusion to address problem behavior at school has increased dramatically since 1970.[1] Among children of color, the increase is especially alarming.[2] Black students are 3.5 times more likely to be

---

1. DANIEL J. LOSEN & RUSSELL SKIBA, SUSPENDED EDUCATION: URBAN MIDDLE SCHOOLS IN CRISIS 2–3 (2011).

2. Tamar Levin, *Black Students Face More Discipline, Data Suggests*, N.Y. TIMES, March 6, 2012, at A11.

suspended than their white peers.[3] Students with disabilities are suspended and expelled at disproportionate rates.[4] The United States Secretary of Education, Arne Duncan, recently asserted that school discipline has become "the civil rights [issue] of our generation."[5]

Two factors explain the dramatic increase in disciplinary exclusion over the last 20 years. First, the emergence of "zero tolerance" policies, which require disciplinary exclusion for first-time problem behavior, has reduced the discretion of school officials to fashion appropriate discipline.[6] Although zero tolerance policies initially related solely to serious misconduct such as possession of firearms, they have been expanded to apply to behavior that used to be addressed by in-school punishment or counseling referrals.[7] Second, tragic school shootings have influenced school officials and policy makers, and led to more reliance on disciplinary exclusion in response to an alleged threat.[8]

Attorneys for students make a difference in school discipline cases because significant procedural and substantive rights protect students against suspension and expulsion. *Goss v. Lopez*[9] established that students have a right to procedural due process in the context of school discipline. At a minimum, students are entitled to notice and the opportunity to be heard when a district suspends or expels. In the context of short-term suspensions, this may only mean a letter home and an informal meeting with the principal to hear the student's side of the story.[10] But for long-term suspension or expulsion, the student has a wide array of rights, including

---

3. LOSEN & SKIBA, *supra* note 1, at 6–7.

4. Donna St. George, *Maryland School Board Moves to Limit Student Suspensions*, WASH. POST, Feb. 28, 2012, at B1.

5. *See* Levin, *supra* note 2.

6. *See generally* Ruth Zweifler & Julia De Beers, *The Children Left Behind: How Zero Tolerance Impacts Our Most Vulnerable Youth*, 8 MICH. J. RACE & L. 191, 194 (2003) (cataloging the spread of mandatory exclusion disciplinary policies to student infractions formerly characterized as "relatively harmless childish pranks").

7. Josie F. Brown, *Developmental Due Process: Waging a Constitutional Campaign to Align School Discipline with Developmental Knowledge*, 82 TEMP. L. REV. 929, 960 (2009).

8. Alicia C. Insley, *Suspending and Expelling Children from Educational Opportunity: Time to Reevaluate Zero Tolerance Policies*, 50 AM. U. L. REV. 1039, 1045 (2001).

9. 419 U.S. 565 (1975).

10. *See id.* at 581.

written notice of the allegations; a hearing prior to imposing the exclusion; counsel; an impartial hearing officer; and the ability to present witnesses and other evidence in the hearing.[11] These procedural rights, however, are meaningless if the student and his family never receive notice of their right to a hearing in the first place, or counsel to help them assert their rights in a hearing. Too many students, like John, need counsel just to get the hearing to which they are entitled.

One procedural safeguard that made a big difference in John's case was the right to cross-examine witnesses. In Washington State, absent some showing that the witness is unavailable or fears retaliation, students are entitled to question and confront witnesses against them.[12] Insisting on the opportunity to question the teacher established two important facts: (1) that the teacher did not really feel threatened by John; and (2) that the teacher did not realize that John had any learning deficits. Had the district been allowed to simply present a summary of the facts from the administrator, the picture presented to the hearing officer would have looked quite different. But again, without counsel, the student and his family would not have been aware of this right, or even known how to raise it as an issue in the hearing.

> **Practice Tip:** Challenge attempts by school districts to have hearings based solely on reports. While the law is not perfectly clear on the right to confront witnesses in discipline hearings, some states have regulations requiring it, and there also is good case law on this issue.

The lawyer also can enforce important substantive limitations on a school district's ability to suspend or expel a student. For example, in John's case,

---

11. Brent Pattison, *Questioning School Discipline: Due Process, Confrontation, and School Discipline Hearings*, 18 TEMP. POL. & CIV. RTS. L. REV. 49, 52 (2008).
12. *See* WASH. ADMIN. CODE § 392-400-270(2)(c) (2006) ("The student and his or her parent(s) or guardian(s) shall have the right to question and confront witnesses, unless a school district witness does not appear and the nonappearance of the witness is excused by the person(s) hearing the case based upon evidence of good reason for doing so submitted by the school district.").

the school district could act only in response to a violation of district policy, and John's attorney used this fact to refocus the hearing to John's benefit. While the school district's attorney focused on the purported zero tolerance approach to threats, he completely ignored a specific district policy spelling out when a threat was significant enough to warrant disciplinary exclusion. John's lawyer was able to refocus the hearing officer's attention on the policy to successfully argue that because John had not violated a school district policy, the district could not expel him.

> **Practice Tip:** Obtain all school district policies related to the allegation and possible disciplinary outcomes. Sometimes the policies are more favorable to students than you might expect, and it is surprising how frequently district officials do not consider them before taking disciplinary action.

In Washington State there are two other important substantive limitations that are not uncommon in other states. First, a student may be suspended or expelled only if the "nature and circumstances of the violation" warrant the disciplinary exclusion.[13] Second, students may not be suspended or expelled for first-time problem misbehavior, except in cases of "exceptional misconduct."[14] In John's case, these two limitations directly conflicted with the school district's reliance on a "zero tolerance" approach to disciplinary exclusion. But it is very unlikely students will be aware of these protections, or how to use them in a hearing, without counsel.

Federal special education law imposes additional substantive limitations on school discipline. Under the Individuals with Disabilities Education

---

13. *See id.* § 392-400-245(1) (setting out limitations on the use of short-term suspensions); § 392-400-260(1) (setting out limitations on the use of long-term suspensions); § 392-400-275(1) (setting out limitations on the use of expulsions).

14. *See, e.g., id.* § 392-400-245(2) ("As a general rule, no student shall be suspended for a short term unless another form of corrective action or punishment reasonably calculated to modify his or her conduct has previously been imposed upon the student as a consequence of misconduct of the same nature. A school district may, however, elect to adopt rules providing for the immediate resort to short-term suspension in cases involving exceptional misconduct…").

Improvement Act (IDEIA)—formerly known and still commonly referred to as the Individuals with Disabilities Education Act or IDEA—and Section 504 of the Rehabilitation Act, students may be removed for more than 10 days only if their behavior is not related to their disability.[15] In addition, under the IDEIA, students have a right to alternative education when suspended or expelled.[16] Even students who are not yet identified as special education students may be entitled to some protection against discipline. A student who the school district knew, or should have known, needed a special education evaluation is entitled to an expedited evaluation and alternative education during the time of the disciplinary exclusion.[17]

> **Practice Tip:** Always investigate whether your client is a special education student, or should be considered for special education. Students with disabilities have important rights when faced with disciplinary exclusion, and the child's special needs may have also influenced the child's behavior.

John's case demonstrates the complicated overlap between school discipline and special education rights. Although John was not eligible for special education at the time of the disciplinary action, his problems in school indicated a possible disability. This required his counsel to investigate whether a previous evaluation had been completed, and whether he might need a new one. Had John already been determined eligible, the school district would have been required to assess whether his behavior was related to his disability and provide alternative education if he was ultimately expelled. But under the circumstances of John's case, the school district was unlikely to provide the family any information about expedited evaluation or alternative services if the family did not have counsel to zealously and creatively advocate for John.

---

15. 20 U.S.C. § 1415(k)(1)(F)(iii) (2004); 34 C.F.R. 104.35(c).
16. 20 U.S.C. § 1415(k)(1)(D)(i).
17. 20 U.S.C. § 1415(k)(5).

John's case also demonstrates the interaction between school discipline and the juvenile delinquency system. Incidents that once were handled in the principal's office are more frequently referred to juvenile courts, leading to what is described as a "school to prison pipeline."[18] Representation for children at disciplinary hearings is a key way to help reverse the pipeline. Without counsel, students may end up getting into more hot water in court. They will probably not be aware that statements they make to school administrators, or in school discipline hearings, may be used against them in juvenile court. Even if they are successful at getting back into school, they may not understand the connection between their school discipline and juvenile offender matters, or how to develop a strategy to address both matters.

---

**Practice Tip:** When there are both school disciplinary proceedings and charges in juvenile court, there needs to be good communication between the lawyers involved. When lawyers collaborate, the child benefits. Juvenile public defenders should consider referring youth for civil legal advocacy when the child has been suspended or expelled as a result of the behavior that led to juvenile court involvement.

---

Having counsel made all the difference between John remaining out of school indefinitely with no educational services, and returning to school with even more support. Counsel's actions on the school front also influenced John's juvenile offender matter, helping him avoid adjudication and a juvenile record. It is not surprising that children and their families have trouble navigating the complicated legal framework relating to school discipline and the intimidating hearing process on their own. Access to counsel balances the scales in these cases, and can radically alter a child's educational opportunities.

---

18. Katherine Burdick, Jessica Feierman & Maura McInerny, *Creating Positive Consequences: Improving Education Outcomes for Youth Adjudicated Delinquent*, 3 DUKE FORUM FOR L. & SOC. CHANGE 5, 7 (2011).

## CHAPTER FIVE

## Setting the Record Straight
# Child Advocacy and School Responses to Mental Health

By Rosa Hirji and Jenny Chau

### PART I: JESSE'S STORY

When a school misperceived a teenage boy's emotional needs and responded to his behaviors with punitive measures, it changed his life trajectory. Instead of receiving appropriate services, the youth was pushed out of his school and eventually ended up in a residential facility. It took an attorney's advocacy to get him home.

Jesse lived in a public housing complex in Los Angeles, California, with his father, mother, and younger brother. His mother was undocumented and could not find work, and thus Jesse's family lived in a constant state of economic and social insecurity. When Jesse was 13 years old, his father died. Jesse began acting out and avoiding school. He also started carrying a knife in his backpack for protection. Even though Jesse was in special education[1] for learning disabilities, the school did not convene an Individualized

---

1. The Individuals with Disabilities Education Improvement Act (IDEIA) is a federal special education law that ensures public schools serve the educational needs of students with disabilities, including the provision of specialized academic instruction and related services they need to benefit from their education. *See* 20 U.S.C. §§ 1400-1482 (2010). The Act was formerly known—and is still commonly referred to—as the Individuals with Disabilities Education Act or IDEA. Under IDEIA, school districts must provide each student with a disability

Education Program (IEP) meeting[2] of his teachers, mother, and counselor to discuss the behavior, nor did the school offer intervention services such as school-based counseling.[3] Instead, Jesse was repeatedly suspended, missing more than thirty days of school in the seventh grade.[4]

One day, Jesse reached out to a school counselor and talked about suicide. The counselor called a psychiatric emergency team. After months of neglecting to identify and support the emotional issues and life stressors that were underlying Jesse's behaviors, the school responded only when Jesse had reached a crisis point. As a result, Jesse was placed on an involuntary psychiatric hold for 72 hours and then detained at a hospital for one week.[5] Jesse was not provided with a representative to contest the detention.[6] Based on a fifteen-minute evaluation at the hospital, a psychiatrist diagnosed Jesse as having bipolar disorder and prescribed a cocktail of strong antipsychotic

---

with a free and appropriate public education (FAPE) in the least restrictive environment. *See* 34 C.F.R. § 300.114 (2006).

2. An IEP is a written statement for each child with a disability that includes the child's present levels of academic achievement and functional performance; measurable annual goals; special education and related services; supplementary aids and services; and program modifications or supports for school personnel to be provided for the child. *See* 20 U.S.C. § 1414(d) and 34 C.F.R. § 300.320. The IEP is developed by the IEP team and must be reviewed at least annually to determine whether the goals for the child are being achieved and revised as appropriate to address any lack of expected progress toward the goals and the general education curriculum. *See* 20 U.S.C. § 1414(d)(3) and 34 C.F.R. § 300.324(b).

3. In developing an IEP, the district must consider special factors. In the case of a child whose behavior impedes the child's learning or that of others, and the district must consider the use of positive behavioral interventions, supports, and other strategies to address the behaviors. *See* 20 U.S.C. § 1414(d)(3) and 34 C.F.R. § 300.324(a)(2). Related services are services that may be required to assist a child with a disability to benefit from his special education, which can include psychological services and mental health services. 34 C.F.R. § 300.34(a) (2006), 20 U.S.C. § 1401(26) (2010).

4. Students with disabilities have procedural protections that are triggered prior to disciplinary actions by the school. *See* 34 C.F.R. § 300.530 (2006).

5. A professional person designated by the county may cause the detention of any person, as a result of his mental disorder, who is a danger to himself or others or is gravely disabled. Cal. Welf. & Inst. Code § 5150 (West 2013).

6. Each person admitted to a designated facility for a 72-hour evaluation and treatment must be informed orally and in writing that he could be held for a longer period of time if the staff decides that he needs continued treatment. If he is held longer than 72 hours, he has a right to a lawyer, a qualified interpreter, and a hearing before a judge. If he is unable to pay for a lawyer, then one is provided for free. Cal. Welf. & Inst. Code § 5157(c) (West 2013). When a person is detained for more than 72 hours, he has the right to contest the legality of his confinement with the state court at any point during his detention by means of "habeas corpus." Cal. Welf. & Inst. Code § 5275 (West 1988).

medications. Jesse was released, but there was no follow up—Jesse did not receive any medical monitoring to evaluate the medication's side effects, nor did he receive any therapy from his school or the psychiatric facility.[7]

Despite being on notice that Jesse was now diagnosed with a mental health condition, the school left him to fend for himself for most of his eighth-grade year. As a side effect of his medications, Jesse experienced hallucinations, talked to himself, told his teachers that he was seeing demons, and fell asleep for hours in the nurse's office. The school continued to suspend Jesse for these behaviors, threatened truancy proceedings,[8] and called the police on a few occasions. The school finally held an IEP meeting—more than a year after Jesse had reached out to the school counselor—and officially recognized Jesse as "emotionally disturbed." The school district then transferred him to yet another school—this time a nonpublic school that served children with behavior problems.

Jesse began his ninth-grade year at his new school. Around this time, Jesse made a decision to stop taking his medications. His bizarre behaviors ceased. School staff acknowledged that Jesse had stabilized and was attending school regularly. This period of stability was abruptly disrupted when personnel at the nonpublic school discovered the knife that Jesse carried in his backpack. Jesse had never used or threatened to use this knife. The nonpublic school stated that they had no choice but to call the police, and referred him for expulsion under their "zero tolerance" policy.[9] The school

---

7. The hospital was required to refer Jesse for further care and treatment, and should have provided Jesse with written or oral information about the probable effects and possible side effects of his medication. Cal. Welf. & Inst. Code § 5152 (2012). Here, Jesse was not provided any medical follow-up.

8. California law establishes the basis and procedures for a referral to a Student Attendance Review Board, an administrative proceeding that could ultimately result in a delinquency referral and/or monetary penalties. Cal. Educ. Code § 48260 *et seq.* (West 2013).

9. California law requires a mandatory expulsion if a student is found to have committed certain enumerated offenses, including "brandishing a knife at another person." Cal. Educ. Code § 48915(c)(2) (West 2013). In Jesse's case, there was no allegation that he brandished the knife. A student who is found in "possession" of a knife has the right to a due process hearing and cannot be expelled unless there is a finding that either (1) other means of correction are not feasible or have repeatedly failed to bring about proper conduct, or (2) due to the nature of the act, the presence of the pupil causes continuing danger to the physical safety of the pupil or others. *Id.* at § 48915(b). Despite the discretionary standards that are written into the law, many schools continue to cite "zero tolerance" as a rationale to justify an automatic removal.

district scheduled an IEP meeting to determine whether Jesse's conduct was a manifestation of his disability.[10]

In the meantime, Jesse was arrested and brought before the juvenile court. The court initiated a psychiatric evaluation. The court-ordered evaluation recounted from Jesse's educational records the disciplinary issues and hallucinations, and cited to the psychiatric hold. The evaluator used these previous records and assessments to support the diagnosis of bipolar disorder, and to conclude that Jesse could not participate in his own defense in the delinquency proceedings. As a result, the court ruled that Jesse was incompetent to stand trial.[11] The juvenile court then appointed an education attorney, separate from his delinquency attorney, to represent Jesse's educational needs.[12] The court instructed the education lawyer to obtain funding from the school district for a residential placement, because the judge wanted an alternative to incarcerating Jesse.[13] If a residential center was located through the school district, the court was inclined to dismiss

---

10. If the district causes a removal of a student with a disability that is considered a change of placement, the district, the parents, and relevant IEP team members must review all relevant information in the student's file and any information provided by the parent to determine if the conduct was caused by, or had a direct and substantial relationship to, the child's disability or if the conduct was a direct result of the district's failure to implement the student's IEP. 34 C.F.R. § 300.530(e) (2006). A change of placement occurs if the removal is for more than 10 consecutive days within a school year. A change of placement also occurs if the student has been subjected to a series of removals that constitute a pattern because the removals total more than 10 days in a school year, the student's behavior was substantially similar to the student's behavior in previous incidents that resulted in the series of removals and because of such additional factors as the length of each removal, the total amount of time the child has been removed, and the proximity of removals to one another. *Id.* section 300.536 (a). If there is a determination that the student's conduct was a manifestation of his disability, the district must not impose disciplinary sanctions on the student and the district is required to continue to provide services pursuant to the student's IEP. *Id.* § 300.530(f).

11. During the pendency of a juvenile proceeding, if the court finds substantial evidence that raises doubt about the minor's competency, the proceedings shall be suspended. Cal. Welf. & Inst. Code § 709(a) (West 2012).

12. If a ward of the court has educational needs that are not being met, the child's attorney may request that the court appoint independent counsel to resolve any education issues outlined in the request. Cal. Welf. & Inst. Code § 317(e) (West 2013).

13. Many courts employ informal resolution and provision of services outside the juvenile justice system for potentially incompetent youth. SUE BURRELL, YOUTH LAW CTR., PROTOCOL FOR COMPETENCE IN CALIFORNIA JUVENILE JUSTICE PROCEEDINGS 4, n.19–20 (Nov. 2012), http://www.ylc.org/wp/wp-content/uploads/Protocol%20with%20Title%20Page.pdf.

the charges.[14] However, there had been no determination that a residential center was a suitable placement for Jesse as opposed to remaining in the community with appropriate supports.

When the education attorney met Jesse, he was 16 years old, slightly short for his age, and sported an earring. They talked about his school experience. Jesse informed his attorney that getting through a school day was an ordeal and often Jesse simply withdrew into his iPod. The attorney noticed that Jesse was restrained when dealing with outside adults and he generally avoided peers at school. She discovered that Jesse, being the oldest male in the family, made major decisions for his family, including educational decisions for his younger brother. Jesse's mother was monolingual Spanish speaking and relied on him to take care of their household needs. Jesse's main concern was whether he had a right to refuse medication because of its side effects. His attorney advised him that he could legally refuse medication.[15] When his attorney also advised him that the juvenile court had appointed her in hopes that she would obtain residential placement for him, Jesse asked her to look into other alternatives. He agreed to participate in a mental health evaluation and consider recommendations made by a professional.

The attorney immediately asked the school district to make a referral for a mental health evaluation, which the district was legally required to perform under the Individuals with Disabilities Education Act (IDEA).[16] The purpose of the evaluation was to determine whether Jesse required mental health services in order to benefit from his education[17] and remain

---

14. *Id.* at 4, n.22 (referring to Los Angeles Superior Court protocol on competency).

15. Several states recognize that minors have a right to consent and to refuse medication and have codified some version of the "Mature Minor Doctrine," a legal principle that allows minors to make decisions about their health and welfare, if they can show they are mature enough to make the decisions on their own. *See generally* A. English & K. Kenny, Ctr. for Adolescent Health & the Law, State Minor Consent Laws: A Summary (2d ed. 2003), for discussion of doctrine. Cal. Code Regs. tit. 15 § 1439(b)(2) (1996) provides that absent an emergency, minors may refuse treatment as it pertains to psychotropic medications.

16. *See* 34 C.F.R. § 300.303 (2006), 20 U.S.C. § 1414(c)(4) (2005).

17. Districts are required to evaluate the student to determine whether the child needs special education and related services. 34 C.F.R. § 300.305(a) (2007), 20 U.S.C. § 1414(c) (2005). Related services are services that assist a child with a disability to benefit from his

in the least restrictive environment.[18] Both Jesse and his attorney hoped that the evaluation would consider that Jesse's behavior had significantly improved and recommend outpatient supports. However, the educationally related mental health evaluation conducted a superficial review of records and relied on interviews of Jesse's previous teachers, who spoke about his period of bizarre behavior, and his probation officer from juvenile court, who urged residential placement. The evaluator did not speak to Jesse and did not administer direct testing. The evaluation affirmed and adopted the previous reports and recommended a residential placement.

Upon the education attorney's request, the school held a two-hour IEP meeting to determine whether Jesse should be placed in residential placement. At the meeting, the education attorney and Jesse's mother questioned whether residential placement was appropriate. They requested school- and community-based mental health supports. During the meeting, Jesse sat with a room full of people talking about him. He whispered to his attorney that he wanted to speak but he was nervous and scared. His attorney asked for a break, and Jesse wrote down his thoughts. In a shaky voice, Jesse read out loud from the piece of paper. He said that he did not deserve to be taken away from his mother, brother, and community and that he would try to do better. Jesse considered this a punishment.

Jesse's mother was torn. She was being counseled by the probation officer that Jesse was at risk of incarceration and a residential placement was the better alternative. She feared that she could not keep him safe in the community and that the school district would continue to involve law enforcement. The school district failed to consider least restrictive alternatives or community-based mental health options. The IEP team recommended that Jesse be sent to a residential placement over the objections of Jesse and his attorney.

---

special education and can include psychological services and mental health services. 34 C.F.R. § 300.34(a) (2006), 20 U.S.C. § 1401(26) (2010).

18. Schools are required to educate children with disabilities with children who are not disabled "to the maximum extent appropriate." A child may be removed from the regular educational setting only if the nature or severity of the disability is such that a child cannot be educated in regular classes, even with the use of supplementary aids and services. 34 C.F.R. § 300.116 (2006), 20 U.S.C. § 1412(a)(5) (2005).

Upon this recommendation, and Jesse's mother's consent, he was sent to the residential center.

To Jesse, residential placement was another form of incarceration. The facility was in a different city and Jesse's mother had to spend hours on public transportation to visit him. As a consequence, Jesse was unable to see his family regularly. Jesse struggled with facility staff who pressured him to take medication that he did not want to take. He did not exhibit behavioral problems, and the facility staff sent home positive reports. Jesse repeatedly asked his attorney to try to get him out of the placement.

Jesse's attorney knew that if Jesse's mother removed him, it would be "against medical advice," and that the school district could obtain an order for residential placement.[19] There also was the risk that the juvenile court would detain him if the court found that removal from the residential facility was not in Jesse's best interests.

The attorney requested and carefully scoured Jesse's past education and mental health records, looking especially at whether the current mental health evaluation had been done in accordance with the law; she found that it had not been.[20] The attorney fought to obtain funding from the school district for an independent educationally related mental health evaluation,[21] but it took months.[22] During that time, Jesse was assaulted in the residen-

---

19. If the district determined that the residential facility was necessary to provide a free and appropriate public education and Jesse's mother did not consent to the placement, the district would have had to initiate a due process hearing. *See* Cal. Educ. Code section 56346(f) (West 2013).

20. In conducting the evaluation, the school district failed to use a variety of assessment tools and strategies to gather relevant functional, developmental, and academic information about the child. It also failed to use testing instruments to assess the relative contribution of cognitive and behavioral factors, in addition to physical and developmental factors, and instead used interviews as a sole criterion for determining that residential placement was appropriate. *See* 34 C.F.R. § 300.304 (2006).

21. If a parent disagrees with the school district's assessments, the parent has a right to request an independent educational evaluation (IEE) at public expense. 34 C.F.R. § 300.502(b) (2006).

22. If a parent requests an IEE at public expense, the school district must, without unnecessary delay, either file a due process complaint to request a hearing to show that its evaluation is appropriate, or ensure that the IEE will be provided at public expense. 34 C.F.R. § 300.502(b) (2) (2006). Whether a delay is unreasonable will turn on the facts of the case. *See, e.g.,* Student v. Los Angeles Unified School District, OAH Case No. 2011020188. There, the Office of Administrative Hearings in California found that a ninety-day delay in denying a parent

tial placement. He also faced tremendous pressure to take his medications, including being threatened with being placed in a more secure facility. Once the independent evaluation was finally approved by the school district, the residential placement prevented the independent evaluator from entering their facility, for fear of legal exposure. Only after the education attorney threatened the school district that she would obtain an order from a hearing officer,[23] the independent evaluator—who had no ties to the school district or probation—finally gained access to Jesse. The evaluator met with Jesse on several occasions to conduct the comprehensive testing, observed him in his placement, interviewed his mother, interviewed Jesse's teachers, and reviewed his entire educational and mental health files.

---

**Practice Tip:** As in Jesse's case, files rarely accompany the child who is transferred between agencies unless there is an advocate that facilitates this. Education attorneys spend a significant amount of time collecting records, and may, at times, have to initiate compliance proceedings to enforce the child's right to records. Providing the evaluator with a comprehensive and organized file of all copies of educational, mental health, and other relevant records for the child will ensure a more thorough evaluation.

---

The results of the independent evaluation were shocking. First, the evaluator found that there was no evidence that Jesse had a bipolar disorder. He found, however, that Jesse was depressed and exhibited an Attention Deficit Hyperactivity Disorder (ADHD). The evaluator concluded that the previous evaluations had misdiagnosed Jesse with bipolar disorder because they relied on an inaccurate history and repeated the previous diagnosis. The

---

request for a publicly funded IEE was unreasonable given the district's failure to communicate with the parents during the time or explain the reason for the delay.

23. An independent evaluator shall have an equivalent opportunity to observe the student in the student's current educational placement and setting if the district observed the student in conducting its assessments, or if its assessment procedures make it permissible to have in-class observations of the pupil. *See* Cal. Educ. Code § 56329(c).

evaluator was concerned that the school and other past providers had not adequately accounted for the social stressors in Jesse's life, had failed to identify a severe hearing impairment, and had not adequately addressed his learning disabilities. Had no one uncovered the fact that Jesse was practically deaf in one ear, asked the evaluator? That Jesse was reading and writing at the third-grade level? The evaluation concluded that Jesse required serious academic intervention and mental health counseling that could be delivered in the community, and there was no need for residential placement.

With the independent evaluation, Jesse's attorney filed a special education due process hearing request, in an effort to change his placement from the residential facility and return him to the community with comprehensive services.[24] As part of the process, the school district and Jesse's mother attended mediation. Jesse also was present. The school district agreed to enter into a settlement agreement in which they would provide community-based counseling and academic intervention as a form of compensatory services for their failure to provide an appropriate evaluation, and failure to educate Jesse in the least restrictive environment. They also agreed to place him in a nonpublic school close to his home. Jesse and his mother agreed to withdraw their due process request.

Jesse returned to his home and community, where his difficult life circumstances remained unchanged. While the school placement was changed, the school district did not fulfill its promise to provide the compensatory services, causing his education attorney to file a complaint with the state department of education to enforce the settlement agreement.[25] It took more than a year to obtain the services. In the meantime, Jesse continued to struggle, academically and socially.

---

24. A parent may initiate due process proceedings if the public agency refuses to initiate or change the identification, assessment, or educational placement. *See* 34 C.F.R. § 300.507 (2006); 20 U.S.C. § 1415(b)(6) (2005).

25. Ultimately, the state department of education is responsible for ensuring that required procedures are followed and that students receive needed education services in accordance with their IEPs. *See* 34 C.F.R. § 300.600 (2008). Violations of the IDEIA must be investigated by the state department of education and a written decision shall be issued to the complainant within sixty days. 34 C.F.R. § 300.152(a) (2006); Cal. Educ. Code § 56500.2 (West 2007) (implementing requirements under 34 C.F.R. § 300.152).

The next school year, the school district conducted another evaluation and reaffirmed its position that Jesse was emotionally disturbed. The independent evaluation that Jesse had fought so hard to obtain was ignored because it criticized the school district.[26] At that point, Jesse, then 17 years old, was close to graduation age but was so behind in credits that it was unlikely he would be able to gain his high school diploma.

## PART II: SCHOOLS, SPECIAL EDUCATION, AND MENTAL HEALTH ISSUES

Jesse's problems—including his family's precarious economic situation, his mother's undocumented status, the dangers of living in the projects, and his own learning disabilities—were complex. His problems were related to his individual needs, but they were also the result of the socioeconomic conditions his family and community found themselves in. When he reached a crisis, his school should have been the first point of intervention. Instead, he was pushed out of his school and into the juvenile delinquency system. These institutions focused their efforts on "reforming" Jesse without accounting for factors beyond his control. They ultimately failed because after returning from institutionalization, Jesse's life circumstances were unchanged and he was in a worse position to cope with them.

Many youth spend most of their waking hours in school. Therefore, schools are the primary institution—aside from the family—to identify mental illness, or the need for intervention to address medical, social, or behavioral needs. Under federal law, Jesse had the right to school-based mental health support to keep him in the least restrictive environment and a right to not face disciplinary sanctions for behaviors that were a manifestation of his disability.[27] The school was required by law to address his

---

26. The law requires that districts consider the results of publicly funded or privately funded evaluations obtained by parents when making decisions involving the provision of a FAPE to the child. 34 C.F.R. § 300.502(c)(1) (2006). While the district has an obligation to consider the results of an IEE, it has no obligation to adopt the evaluator's recommendations or conclusions. *See, e.g.,* T.S. v. Board of Educ. of the Town of Ridgefield, 10 F.3d 87 (2d Cir. 1993); G.D. v. Westmoreland Sch. Dist., 930 F.2d 942 (1st Cir. 1991); Student v. Garvey Sch. Dist., OAH Case Nos. 2010011021 and 2010030772.

27. *See supra* note 10.

needs and had a myriad of approaches available, including wraparound support, positive behavior intervention, counseling, and referrals to community services.[28]

Instead, Jesse's school responded with punitive measures, causing him to become intertwined with the delinquency system and mental health agencies. These entities have a mandate to act in "the child's best interest," but ultimately they set Jesse on a trajectory that unnecessarily relied on medication and institutionalization in an unsuccessful attempt to address Jesse's needs. Each time one of these institutions "processed" Jesse, it relied on the last institution's documentation of his needs, and then he was further stripped of his rights to dictate his future. After his father died, Jesse started acting out and missing school. But the school never put together a new IEP to provide Jesse with community-based mental health services. Such services could have kept Jesse at home and in his local school—the least restrictive environment. Without such services, Jesse decompensated. By the time Jesse reached a crisis point, perhaps the school had no choice but to set the process in motion that eventually led to the involuntary hold. However, the efficacy of the decision was later questioned by Jesse's independent evaluator. During the detention in the psychiatric hospital, Jesse did not have access to an attorney, and he was provided with a superficial psychiatric evaluation that diagnosed him with a major mood disorder. Through the juvenile court and its evaluation process, he was deemed incompetent and thereafter was unable to challenge the charges against him. The school district conducted its own evaluation that not only failed to comply with the requirements under the law, but also failed to include the child's input and

---

28. The district should have developed a behavior intervention plan. The law requires districts to develop and implement a behavior intervention plan when a student with a disability commits an act of misconduct that is determined to be a manifestation of his disability. *See* 34 C.F.R. § 300.530(f) (2006). If a student with exceptional needs is identified as requiring mental health services, the district shall provide specially designed instruction required by the student's IEP, including related services such as counseling services, parent counseling and training, psychological services, or social work services in school. If the district is not able to provide appropriate mental health services for the student, the district may refer the student to a community mental health service in accordance with Cal. Gov't Code § 7576. Cal. Educ. Code § 56331. This provision was repealed by the California State Legislature on July 1, 2011; however, the IDEIA still requires school districts to provide mental health services if necessary for the child to benefit from his education.

acknowledge his life circumstances. The school district ignored significant factors that indicated that Jesse did not need to be institutionalized and instead could be effectively served in his community.

> **Practice Tip:** The child's attorney should view all prior "best interest" determinations, in their various contexts, with an open mind. Develop a case chronology and review this with the parent and the child to obtain their perspective. Attorneys who represent children with mental health needs should attempt to gain familiarity with various forms of mental health evaluations to make an initial determination of whether they were comprehensive, whether they were used for the purposes and manner they were designed for, and whether they met appropriate legal standards for the tribunal that eventually relied on them. In most cases, it is critical to obtain an independent evaluation to help guide the attorney and child in obtaining appropriate services, challenging previous decisions, and constructing remedies.

No system can work in the best interest of the child when it ignores the interests of the child himself and the conditions that he is forced to live with. However, our approach to mental health and juvenile delinquency is designed to treat the types of problems Jesse faced as an individual disorder with the focus being entirely on modifying the child's behavior; there is no attempt to question or address the social, economic, educational, environmental, and cultural differences or conditions that exist beyond the child's control.[29] In this case, it is highly likely that Jesse fell victim to a well-documented tendency to overdiagnose poor children with psychiatric illnesses and to overprescribe antipsychotic medications.[30] Indeed, the

---

29. *See* PETER R. BREGGIN, M.D. & GINGER ROSS BREGGIN, THE WAR AGAINST CHILDREN OF COLOR: PSYCHIATRY TARGETS INNER CITY YOUTH (1998).

30. A Rutgers-Columbia study published in *Health Affairs* in 2009 found that Medicaid-enrolled children are prescribed antipsychotic drugs at a rate four times higher than those children whose parents have private insurance, and that children enrolled in Medicaid are also more likely to receive the drugs for less severe conditions than their middle-class counterparts. *See* Stephan Crystal et al., *Broadened Use of Atypical Antipsychotics: Safety, Effectiveness, and*

approach to mental health in the United States in the last two decades is illustrated by the skyrocketing rate of psychopharmacological interventions for children, coinciding with decreased investment in community-based mental health.[31]

In Jesse's case, the juvenile court and school district viewed residential care as an appropriate and effective alternative to a child living in traumatic conditions and attending a failing school. These agencies failed to consider less restrictive alternatives for Jesse. Less restrictive alternatives to residential treatment include, but are not limited to, integrated community-based services, including case management and wraparound services; and in-home community-based services, including multisystemic therapy, functional family therapy, assertive community treatment, and mentoring.[32] Studies have shown that these alternatives to residential treatment are effective and have better clinical outcomes,[33] and that families and youth benefit when youth remain in the communities while receiving therapeutic services.[34]

However, even if the court, school district, and mental health agencies had considered the alternatives already available, these institutions are not empowered to challenge systemic issues related to the manner in which our society responds to children who come from low-income and disadvantaged

---

*Policy Challenges*, HEALTH AFF. (July 2009), *available at* http://www.ncbi.nlm.nih.gov/pmc/articles/PMC2896705/; Duff Wilson, *Poor Children Likelier to Get Antipsychotics*, N.Y. TIMES, Dec. 11, 2009, http://www.nytimes.com/2009/12/12/health/12medicaid.html?pagewanted=all &_r=0. A print version of the article appeared in the NY Times on Dec. 12, 2009 on A1 of the New York edition. New studies have revealed that children in foster care are more likely to be prescribed antipsychotic medication than the disabled population in general, even though the disorders that these medications are designed to treat—for example, bipolar disorder and schizophrenia—are extremely rare; they receive psychiatric medication at twice the rate of the general population. Benedict Carey, *Drugs Used for Psychotics Go to Youths in Foster Care*, N.Y. TIMES, Nov. 20, 2011, http://www.nytimes.com/2011/11/21/health/research/study-finds-foster-children-often-given-antipsychosis-drugs.html. This article appeared in print on Nov. 21, 2011 on page A13 of the New York edition with the headline "Drugs Used for Psychosis Go to Youths in Foster Care."

31. ROBERT WHITAKER, ANATOMY OF AN EPIDEMIC: MAGIC BULLETS, PSYCHIATRIC DRUGS, AND THE ASTONISHING RISE OF MENTAL ILLNESS IN AMERICA 243–45 (2010).

32. MAGELLAN HEALTH SERV. CHILD. SERV. TASK FORCE, PERSPECTIVES ON RESIDENTIAL AND COMMUNITY-BASED TREATMENT FOR YOUTH AND FAMILIES 8–10 (2008).

33. *Id.* at 11.

34. Melanie B. Sullivan et al., *Family Centered Treatment—An Alternative to Residential Placements for Adjudicated Youth: Outcomes and Cost-Effectiveness*, J. OF JUV. JUST., Fall 2012, at 25.

communities. The glaring fact that Jesse would never have been detained or arrested had he come from a middle-class, English-speaking family (because his family would have privately paid for therapy and he would not have had added stressors in his life) was totally ignored.

Yet, notwithstanding the number of less restrictive therapeutic alternatives, the school district instead placed Jesse in residential care, which is the second most restrictive and costly treatment for children and adolescents, next to inpatient psychiatric hospitalization.[35] Jesse's mother, who had the legal authority to approve the placement, was pressured to consent to the placement or to face other consequences such as detention by the juvenile court. Research demonstrates that youth in residential treatment "make gains between admission and discharge, but many do not maintain improvement post-discharge."[36] A survey of literature demonstrates that "gains made during a stay in residential treatment may not transfer well back to the youth's natural environment" and that such treatment may create "a cycle where children are repeatedly readmitted."[37] In one study, parents in focus groups said that after only a few months, their children were readmitted to residential treatment or entered the justice system due to lack of services in the community or lack of coordination with community supports, or because their children did not have the skills needed to succeed in the community.[38] Indeed, this related directly to Jesse's experience. Jesse's placement in the restrictive setting not only deprived him of his right to be educated in the least restrictive environment, but it failed to provide him with the tools to succeed upon returning to his community.

It is not up to the attorney to question the medical and psychiatric judgment of professionals. But it is the attorney's obligation to do so if there is reason to suspect that judgment is impaired by a failure to comply with standards of care in the law or a tendency of institutions to institutionalize

---

35. MAGELLAN HEALTH SERV. CHILD. SERV. TASK FORCE, PERSPECTIVES ON RESIDENTIAL AND COMMUNITY-BASED TREATMENT FOR YOUTH AND FAMILIES 4 (2008).

36. *Id.* at 4 (citing B.J. Burns et al., *Effective Treatment for Mental Disorders in Children and Adolescents*, 2 CLINICAL CHILD AND FAM. PSYCHOL. REV., no. 4, 1999, at 199).

37. *Id.* (citing MERCER GOV'T HUM. SERV. CONSULTING, WHITE PAPER COMMUNITY ALTERNATIVES TO PSYCHIATRIC RESIDENTIAL TREATMENT FACILITY SERVICES (2008)).

38. *Id.* at 5.

or medicate as a form of behavioral control; or when specifically directed by her client. In this case, the role of the attorney centered on obtaining an independent evaluation that eventually supported what Jesse and his mother suspected. The success in obtaining the evaluation was hindered by the amount of time it took and the fact that it did not result in long-term solutions to Jesse's problems.

---

**Practice Tip**: Child advocates should combine individual advocacy efforts with strategies to combat long-term institutional problems that impact their clients. Such strategies include educating the public and policy makers about their findings, participating in efforts to change or influence law and policy, and engaging with community-based organizations that work to mobilize local communities around the issues that they face. This type of involvement requires the attorney to develop a critical perspective on laws and can only be done by reading about the issues and talking to different stakeholders.

---

A child's attorney can and should challenge the best-interest determinations of the institutions that play a controlling role in the child's liberty and other interests, when the determination is improper or when it does not coincide with the actual interest of the child. But unless we as a society address the conditions that cause a childhood of insecurity and trauma in the first place, and respond to behaviors in children that are symptomatic of both their external and internal challenges with a compassionate, nonpunitive approach, we will only win battles but eventually lose the war. And unless child advocates participate in efforts for systemic change, the war will never be fought. In Jesse's case, his lawyer was able only to return him to the conditions that caused his behaviors and emotional needs in the first instance. Jesse and his lawyer continue to search for community and school-based supports. Jesse is happy to be home with his family.

# CHAPTER SIX

## A Matter of Survival
# Representing Runaway and Homeless Youth

By Casey Trupin

### PART I: SAMMY'S STORY

Police brought 16-year-old Sammy to Spruce Street Secure Crisis Residential Center, a short-term lockdown facility in Seattle, Washington, for runaways, after he ran away from home. Most youth at Spruce Street are ultimately sent home to their families, so it came as no surprise when the state's Children's Administration (CA) ordered the facility to return Sammy to his caretaker. But Spruce Street's program director, who had a gut feeling that something was amiss and was uneasy about sending Sammy home, reached out to the Street Youth Legal Advocates of Washington (SYLAW) for help. SYLAW spent the better part of a year fighting for Sammy—often against the very agency that was charged with promoting his well-being— to secure a safe and stable home for him.

SYLAW's first step was to interview Sammy, who described a life of horrors, every bit of which and more was confirmed by SYLAW's investigation. When Sammy and his twin brother, Billy, were toddlers, their mother disappeared and subsequently died from an overdose. Then their father went to prison. Still toddlers, the two boys ended up in the care of a family friend, Frida, who lived with her adult daughter, Julie. During the time that Sammy and Billy lived with Frida and Julie, CA received dozens of referrals and conducted sixteen intakes on the family. The agency received calls from concerned teachers, counselors, neighbors, family friends, and the police—many indicating possible abuse by Julie. The allegations of abuse were severe, including threats to cut off the boys' penises and nail them to the wall, striking their heads against the table corner, beatings with kitchen utensils, black eyes, lacerations, choking, starving, and other assaults. Their caretakers threatened the boys with starvation if they told anyone of the abuse, so the boys lied, though not always convincingly. The lies were as transparent as blaming rabbit attacks for their cuts and marks. Frida and Julie often kept the boys home from school when they had bruises, or moved the boys from one school to another. Frida once threatened a school with a lawsuit for harassment if the school continued to interfere.

Over the years, CA passed the boys off from one caseworker to another and among different divisions. But each caseworker would eventually just close the case without providing any protection to the boys or finding them a new placement. CA's own notes indicate that the agency closed the case once because Frida threatened legal action against CA. Twice, CA's records noted allegations that Frida and/or Julie personally knew a CA worker who was tipping them off before investigations, but CA never followed up on the allegation. Inexplicably, caseworkers would often rate the risk to the boys as low, despite the number of allegations and concerns that the boys were small for their age and unable to fend for themselves.

When the boys were teenagers, Frida passed away, leaving the twins in the sole care of Julie. The abuse continued. When the boys were 16, Julie admitted to a police officer that she had physically assaulted Sammy on a number of occasions—she had backhanded him so hard his nose bled, thrown him five feet onto a couch, pulled his hair, punched him in the chest with a closed fist, thrown food at him, backhanded him while wearing rings, and hit him with a telephone. She also admitted that she had forced Sammy to steal for her on 25 occasions. If she were the officer, she told him, she would be "disgusted" with herself. The thefts, it turned out, were to support Julie's substance abuse. CA received this report, but never took action on it, still insisting that the boys be returned to Julie's care.

Over the years, both boys took to the streets to escape the abuse. Billy would get himself locked up in juvenile detention and hide in abandoned buildings. And Sammy would try to get locked up at Spruce Street, a facility that other runaway youth were desperately trying to escape.

SYLAW's advocacy on Sammy's behalf met CA's opposition from the start. Indeed, CA attempted to retaliate against the Spruce Street program director for referring Sammy and letting him speak to his attorney; the agency argued that Sammy had no right to talk to his attorney even after Sammy specifically asked the attorney for help.

One of SYLAW's first tasks was to convince CA that neither Frida, who was deceased, nor her daughter Julie was related to Sammy and his brother, and that the women had never obtained legal custody of the boys. CA's notes indicated massive confusion about Frida's identity; at times the agency mistook her for the boys' biological mother and insisted that Julie was a stepsister. SYLAW attempted to clear up the confusion, explaining the lack of a legal relationship and showing that petitions by Frida and Julie for legal custody and guardianship had been dismissed. Despite this, CA continued to take the position that these boys should be returned to Julie's care, explaining that it "took [Julie] at her word" that she was the legal guardian.

Sammy had been in touch with Brian, the brother of an ex-boyfriend of Julie's. When interviewed by SYLAW, Brian corroborated the allegations of Julie's abusive behavior, and was very concerned about the twins' welfare. Brian stepped up and agreed to take custody of Sammy for as long as necessary. Brian filed a petition to establish nonparental custody and make Brian Sammy's legal custodian. (Billy had not yet contacted SYLAW.)

At the preliminary hearing, Julie appeared and argued that she had legal custody of the boys; she said her "proof" was that the state was giving her food stamps and medical coupons for their care. SYLAW argued that she had no legal relationship to the boys, and that the state's decision to provide her with public benefits for the boys did not alter that fact. SYLAW successfully asserted that the only living adult with any rights to the boys was their incarcerated father, whom SYLAW had tracked down in prison. He had become a model prisoner, and explained that his efforts to locate Sammy and Billy had been futile, as Frida and Julie had kept them hidden. The father agreed to help wrest legal control of the children from Julie, by supporting Sammy's request to live with Brian.

The judge sided with Sammy. First, the court found that Julie lacked standing and dramatically ordered her to leave the courtroom to allow the confidential hearing to proceed. Julie left and was not heard from again. The court then granted legal custody of Sammy to Brian, with Sammy's father having the right to stay involved with Sammy. Once the court determined that Julie was not a legal parent, Billy felt free not to return to Julie's care. He later joined Sammy. After their father was released from prison, Brian helped him reunite with Sammy and Billy. The children, in fact, began living with their father again, with Brian's support.

Even after the family court excluded Julie from the case because she lacked standing and ordered Sammy into Brian's care, CA continued to argue for Sammy's return to Julie. In all the years that the CA received abuse allegations, the agency never once removed the boys from their home, and instead actively fought the attempts of Spruce Street staff, the boys' friends, and Sammy's attorney to put an end to the abuse. Without the intervention of an attorney, there would have been no possibility to achieve what Sammy ultimately found—a stable and happy home with his twin brother and father.

## PART II: ADVOCATING FOR HOMELESS AND RUNAWAY YOUTH

Characteristics of Homeless and Runaway Youth

The National Alliance to End Homelessness (NAEH) estimates that 550,000 youth like Sammy experience homelessness each year.[1] Schools reported almost 53,000 unaccompanied homeless youth in the 2008–2009 school year. A similar number of youth used homeless youth services in 2007.[2] These youth often flee homes in which they experience physical and/or sexual abuse.[3] While infant victims account for most homicides, a

---

1. NAT'L NETWORK FOR YOUTH, RUNAWAY AND HOMELESS YOUTH ACT FACT SHEET, *available at* http://www.nn4youth.org/system/files/NN4Y%20RHYA%20Fact%20Sheet%20%282013%29.pdf.

2. *Id.*; U.S. Interagency Council on Homelessness, *Opening Doors: Federal Strategic Plan to Prevent and End Homelessness* 15 (2010), *available at* http://usich.gov/PDF/OpeningDoors_2010_FSPPreventEndHomeless.pdf.

3. It is estimated that 17%–35% of homeless and runaway youth have been subject to sexual abuse. *See* Marjorie J. Robertson & Paul A. Toro, *Homeless Youth: Research, Intervention, and Policy, in* PRACTICAL LESSONS: THE 1998 NATIONAL SYMPOSIUM ON HOMELESSNESS

study in the *Journal of the American Medical Association* reported that the "overall incidence of abuse and neglect in adolescents is either higher or the same as that of younger children."[4] Most new reports of maltreatment occur disproportionately among older children and adolescents, yet older children are more likely to be perceived as responsible for their own maltreatment.[5] Homeless youth often come from families with high rates of parental drug or alcohol abuse.[6] More than one in five youth who age out of foster care experience at least one day of homelessness within a year of leaving care.[7] Additionally, as many as 255,000 youth age out of the juvenile justice system each year.[8]

Living in shelters or on the streets, unaccompanied homeless youth are at high risk for physical and sexual assault or abuse and physical illness, including HIV/AIDS. Homeless youth also face a high likelihood of becoming involved in prostitution. This is on top of the wide range of serious risk behaviors that adolescents may engage in as a result of their past maltreatment, including premature sexual activity, unintended pregnancy, emotional disorders, suicide attempts, eating disorders, alcohol and drug abuse, and delinquent behavior.[9]

Despite all of these setbacks, many homeless youth remain in school. A 2005 survey found that before entering shelter, 79% of homeless youth regularly attended school, and 78% of youth in transitional housing were still in school.[10]

---

RESEARCH 3-8 (Linda B. Fosburg & Deborah L. Dennis eds.), *available at* http://www.eric.ed .gov/PDFS/ED443892.pdf.

4. Council on Scientific Affairs, Am. Med. Ass'n, *Adolescents as Victims of Family Violence*, 270 JAMA 1850, 1850 (1993).

5. *Id.* at 1852.

6. Robertson & Toro, *supra* note 3, at 3-12.

7. PETER PECORA ET AL., IMPROVING FOSTER FAMILY CARE: FINDINGS FROM THE NORTHWEST FOSTER CARE ALUMNI STUDY 37 (2005), *available at* http://www.casey.org/Resources/ Publications/pdf/ImprovingFamilyFosterCare_FR.pdf.

8. U.S. INTERAGENCY COUNCIL ON HOMELESSNESS, OPENING DOORS: FEDERAL STRATEGIC PLAN TO PREVENT AND END HOMELESSNESS: HOMELESSNESS AMONG YOUTH (2010), *available at* http://www.usich.gov/resources/uploads/asset_library/FactSheetYouth.pdf.

9. Robertson & Toro, *supra* note 3, at 3-10-3-14.

10. NAT'L ALLIANCE TO END HOMELESSNESS, FACT SHEET: YOUTH HOMELESSNESS 2 (2010), *available at* http://b.3cdn.net/naeh/7947d5ba7cdd6c309f_bdm6bxt27.pdf.

Youth who are homeless are more likely to turn to low-level offenses—petty theft, other property offenses, and drug-related offenses—to survive. Unaccompanied youth are at a distinct disadvantage in juvenile court proceedings. Not only are they unlikely to have an effective parent advocate, they may, in fact, have a parent who wants the youth to be locked up. It is not uncommon for a homeless youth to be charged because of a domestic altercation with the child's parents. Without a parent on his or her side to advise him or her, the youth may take a bad plea deal, or not sufficiently consider longer-term collateral consequences. If locked up, the youth may have no parent to be released to when the court is ready to discharge him or her, and thus could end up spending more time in detention. Lacking a stable place to live, homeless youth who are on probation may be unable to comply with such conditions as regular check-ins, or may be placed on electronic monitoring as an alternative to detention.

## Options for Homeless and Runaway Youth

When physical or sexual abuse or extreme neglect caused the youth's homelessness, instituting abuse and neglect (dependency or deprivation) proceedings is one strategy to address the family's issues. However, many child welfare agencies are reluctant to institute such cases for older youth; consequently, those youth are more likely to become involved with the juvenile justice or status offense systems. Sammy's case is an excellent example of this. Dozens of referrals and numerous investigations had already taken place before SYLAW ever got the case. Sammy's brother Billy might never have been involved with the juvenile justice system if the child welfare system had taken action.

Status offenses are quasi-criminal offenses that would not be actionable if they were committed by adults. Compared to other types of juvenile legal proceedings, status offense proceedings provide some benefits to homeless youth, yet they can generate detrimental effects as well.

Status offenses vary tremendously from state to state. However, the most common process—known as a FINS (Family in Need of Services), CHINS (Child in Need of Services), or some variation thereof depending on the state—provides the court with some level of control over the child's (and, to a lesser extent, the family's) behavior. In some states, the court's order to the family members to behave in a certain manner carries with it the possibility of contempt, and even the threat of detention of the youth, upon violation. Depending on the state, the child may be ordered to live in an out-of-home placement, which, for a homeless youth, could temporarily resolve a housing dilemma. However, some states rely on quasi-criminal group homes for status offenders, which may not resolve long-term familial issues that prompted the youth's homelessness. Rarely, in some states, a youth can file his or her own status offense petition with the court to request out-of-home care. For example, Sammy could have filed a petition that he was a Child in Need of Services,[11] by which he could ask the court to order him placed in someone's home. For Sammy, however, the fact that there was no legal guardian against whom to file may have precluded this approach. Importantly, housing options for a youth in status offense proceedings will typically be broader than those in abuse and neglect proceedings, as these youth are not generally required to live in a licensed foster care home or relative placement. In addition to housing, status offense proceedings can open doors to other beneficial services—assistance from a caseworker, and mental health and substance use counseling.

On the flip side, status offenses can set a youth up for unnecessary involvement in or scrutiny by the juvenile justice system. A youth who runs from a placement (or otherwise violates a court order) may face civil or criminal contempt of court. As compared to a youth involved in abuse and neglect proceedings, a status offender may not have access to as broad a range of placements or services, or postmajority support.

Emancipation sometimes may be another route for a youth to escape an abusive parent. This proceeding, created either through common law or statute, provides youth with the ability to enter into a binding lease and exercise other rights usually reserved for adults. About one-half of the states have a statutorily codified option for emancipation.[12] Emancipation, however, is a legal catch-22. A youth generally has to show that he or she can support himself or herself to be legally emancipated, a high hurdle for

---

11. Wash. Rev. Code § 13.32a.160 (2000).

12. *Emancipation of Minors—Laws*, Legal Information Institute, http://www.law.cornell.edu/wex/table_emancipation.

a youth who has been deprived of emotional or financial support from his or her parents.

## Current Role of the Federal Government

The federal government has created modest funding streams designed to prevent and end youth homelessness. The Runaway and Homeless Youth Act helps fund local programs to serve hundreds of thousands of homeless and runaway youth.[13] Still, not all youth who need shelter and housing can access this life essential—in 2008, the Department of Health and Human Services reported more than 7,663 homeless and runaway youth were turned away from shelters due to lack of bed spaces.[14]

The Chafee Foster Care Independence Program (CFCIP) provides funding to support youth who are expected to or who do age out of the foster care system.[15] In addition, as a result of the federal Fostering Connections to Success Act, states may receive federal financial support if they choose to allow youth to stay in foster care until age 21.[16]

Most unaccompanied minors continue to be, or at least want to be, connected to their school. The federal McKinney-Vento Homeless Assistance Act, first passed in 1987 and since reauthorized several times, provides protections for homeless children and youth to ensure that they receive the same quality of education as housed students. McKinney-Vento addresses many of the obstacles that homeless students face in pursuing their education and directs school districts to ensure that homeless children are not discriminated against in the classroom or with respect to enrollment, transportation, full access, and other services.[17] Most critically, the act requires school districts

---

13. 42 U.S.C. §§ 5711–14 (2003).

14. Nat'l Network for Youth, Statement for the Record before the Subcommittee on Labor, Health and Human Services, Committee on Appropriations, U.S. House of Representatives (2008).

15. See John H. Chaffee Foster Care Independence Program, U.S. DEP'T OF HEALTH & HUM. SERV., CHILD. BUREAU (June 28, 2012), http://www.acf.hhs.gov/programs/cb/resource/chafee-foster-care-program.

16. Fostering Connections to Success and Increasing Adoptions Act of 2008, Pub. L. No. 110-351, 122 Stat. 3949. For more information, see http://www.nrcpfc.org/fostering_connections/.

17. The act defines homeless youth as those "who lack a fixed, regular, and adequate nighttime residence" and lists various examples of children who are considered homeless. 42

to allow homeless students to remain in their school of origin—that is, the school they attended before becoming homeless—or to enroll in a school that other students living in the attendance area are allowed to attend.[18] (See Box 2, "Major Federal Laws Affecting Homeless Youth.")

Youth such as Sammy are likely to come into contact with one legal system or another—even those who do not have their life choices and outcomes dictated by a web of laws that are as likely to keep them homeless as they are to aid them in their exit from the streets.

## Advocacy Efforts for Systemic Reform

Legislative, litigation, and legal education efforts to help youth such as Sammy on a broad scale are taking place throughout the nation. (See Box 1, "Resources for Lawyers Working with Homeless Youth.")

**Law reform.** State laws affecting homeless youth are extremely varied. The National Law Center on Homelessness and Poverty and the National Network for Youth (NN4Y) have catalogued the major state laws affecting this population.[19] In 2009, the American Bar Association's Commission on Homelessness and Poverty and NN4Y brought together experts to create RUNAWAY AND HOMELESS YOUTH AND THE LAW: MODEL STATE STATUTES.[20] These and other resources provide a road map to advocates about what legislative reforms are necessary to help youth. Lawyers play a key role in writing and advocating for laws to better address the needs of this population. Local legislative efforts have ranged from extending foster care to age 21 to improving access to education for unaccompanied youth.

**Legal education.** In addition to publishing *Alone without a Home*,[21] lawyers in various states have put together materials to describe, for youth and

---

U.S.C. § 11434a(2)(a) (1994).

18. 42 U.S.C. § 11432(e)(3).

19. NATIONAL LAW CENTER ON HOMELESSNESS AND POVERTY AND NATIONAL NETWORK FOR YOUTH, ALONE WITHOUT A HOME: A STATE BY STATE REVIEW OF LAWS AFFECTING UNACCOMPANIED YOUTH (2012), available at http://www.nlchp.org/Alone_Without_A_Home The National Conference of State Legislatures has also cataloged some of this legislation at http://www.ncsl.org /issues-research /human-services /homeless-and-runaway-youth.aspx.

20. AM. BAR ASS'N COMM. ON HOMELESSNESS & POVERTY, RUNAWAY AND HOMELESS YOUTH AND THE LAW: MODEL STATE STATUTES (2009).

21. JULIANELLE, REEG, ET AL., *supra* note 19.

service providers, information about the existing state of the law. Lack of knowledge around the law has prevented youth from escaping homelessness or has prolonged periods of homelessness. The Law and Corporate Affairs Department at Starbucks, in conjunction with the law firm of Baker & McKenzie and the Washington State legal services agency Columbia Legal Services, created the website homelessyouth.org to increase knowledge about the laws among youth and the professionals who serve them.

**Litigation.** Advocacy groups also have brought litigation to improve conditions for homeless youth. Litigation is often focused on improving outcomes for youth who age out of foster care. For example, the settlement in *Braam v. State*,[22] a class action over conditions in the Washington State foster care system, required the state to "[o]ffer support services to foster youth until age 21" and "propose a statutory change to extend out-of-home care benefits to children through age 21."[23] Similarly, the Legal Aid Society and Lawyers for Children filed *D.B. et al. v. Richter* in New York in 2011 to secure adequate housing for youth before their discharge from foster care.[24]

**Legal clinics.** Finally, in order to serve individual homeless youth for whom legal issues are standing in the way of safety and stability, lawyers have started legal clinics in numerous communities. For example, the Teen Legal Advocacy Project at the University of Connecticut School of Law runs a clinic in Hartford Public Schools that represents homeless youth on a variety of education and civil matters. In Los Angeles, Public Counsel operates a legal clinic at a drop-in center for homeless youth. Similarly, Bay Area Legal Aid operates a clinic at a homeless youth shelter in Oakland.

For youth such as Sammy, legal support is critical to avoid prolonged homelessness, prison, or death. The legal profession has as important a role to play as do the medical and social work professions. Lawyering on behalf

---

22. Braam v. State, 81 P.3d 851 (Wash. 2003).
23. Braam v. State implementation plan, *available at* http://braamkids.org/ImpPlanFeb06 .pdf.
24. D.B. v. Richter, Index No. 402759/11, was settled in March 2012.

of youth in cases that can completely change the trajectory of their lives is at the heart of lawyers' commitment to deliver justice.

## Box 1: Resources for Lawyers Working with Homeless Youth

American Bar Association Homeless Youth and the Law Initiative: http://www.americanbar.org/groups/public_services/homelessness_poverty/ initiatives/homeless_youth_andthelaw.html

American Bar Association Resolution on the Runaway and Homeless Youth Act: http://www.americanbar.org/content/dam/aba/migrated/homeless /PublicDocuments/105B_FINAL.authcheckdam.pdf

Runaway and Homeless Youth and the Law: Model State Statutes (free PDF): http://www.nn4youth.org/system/files/ABA_Runaway_eBook.authcheckdam.pdf

National Law Center on Homelessness and Poverty Children and Youth and Education Program: http://www.nlchp.org/youth

Alone without a Home: A State-by-State Review of Laws Affecting Unaccompanied Youth: http://www.nlchp.org/Alone_Without_A_Home

National Association for the Education of Homeless Children and Youth: www.naehcy.org

National Network for Youth: www.nn4youth.org

## Box 2: Major Federal Laws Affecting Homeless Youth

The Runaway and Homeless Youth Act (RHYA) provides funding for resources for local systems of care for runaway and homeless youth. 42 U.S.C. §§ 5711–14 (2003).

The McKinney-Vento Homeless Assistance Act includes provisions to ensure the enrollment, attendance, and success of homeless children and youth in school. 42 U.S.C. §§ 11431–33 (2002).

The Chafee Foster Care Independence Program provides states with funding to support youth who are likely to and who do age out of foster care. *John H. Chaffee Foster Care Independence Program*, U.S. DEP'T OF HEALTH AND HUMAN SERVICES, CHILDREN'S BUREAU (June 28, 2012), http://www.acf.hhs.gov/programs/cb/resource/chafee-foster-care-program.

The Fostering Connections Act of 2008 offers federal funds to states to extend foster care to youth up until age 21. Pub. L. No. 110-351, 122 Stat. 3949.

# CHAPTER SEVEN

## Getting Another Chance
# Lawyering to Prevent Youth from Being Tried as Adults

By Lourdes M. Rosado with Candace Mitchell

### PART I: TINA'S STORY

Tina was a slight, pimply 17-year-old when she met her attorney for the first time in an adult jail. She had been charged with attempted murder and aggravated assault in adult court as a result of a violent confrontation with her mentally ill mother. Afterward, the police found Tina when she overdosed on her mother's psychotropic medications. For the first three weeks after the incident, she was committed to an inpatient psychiatric facility.

Tina's first meetings with her attorney, Michelle Mason from the Defender's Association in Philadelphia, were challenging. Tina was sometimes catatonic and incoherent, and her youth and mental health issues made it difficult for her to understand why she could not simply return home to her mother. The court had issued a no-contact order between Tina and her mother, so Tina was not only in serious trouble, but also felt totally alone.

Tina's attorney was well aware of the obstacles her client faced in adult court, and wanted to make use of a Pennsylvania law allowing the adult court to "decertify" the case so that Tina could be tried in juvenile court. But decertification out of adult court would be difficult given the violent nature of Tina's case and her age. Tina's attorney realized she needed a multidisciplinary team to help Tina. She enlisted the help of social worker Kia Mayes, as well as a forensic psychologist.

The team began an investigation into Tina's family and social history. They reviewed piles of child welfare and school records. They interviewed teachers and family. What they learned was troubling. Tina lived in a house marked by tension, violence, and mental health problems. Tina had been sexually abused at age six, had experienced physical altercations with her mother, and had been witness to extensive domestic violence. In spite of her exposure to significant trauma, she had had only minimal opportunities for mental health treatment. When she had been committed to facilities, her mother had prematurely discharged her from treatment. Her mother had also failed to provide Tina with the medication she needed to treat her conditions. The local children and youth agency had flitted in and out of her life a couple of times, but provided no real help. In school, Tina had drifted from grade to grade, able to mask her many internal mental and emotional battles with good behavior. As a result, she was not identified as a special education student until she was in the eleventh grade, and even then only because she struggled with mathematics. On the other hand, Tina had strengths: she did not have behavioral problems at school and got along well with her classmates and teachers. Any problems with aggression appeared to be limited to the toxic relationship she had with her mother.

On the mental health side, old psychological and psychiatric evaluations with multiple "rule outs" of possible disorders gave no clear, current picture of Tina's needs. So Tina's defense team arranged for a complete psychological evaluation. The evaluation revealed that Tina had untreated bipolar disorder. The legal team also explored questions of competence and a possible insanity defense with the forensic evaluator, but eventually concluded that these were not applicable in Tina's case.

In her decertification hearing, the legal team told Tina's story of missed opportunities for help. They explained her troubled childhood, exposure to trauma, and mental health history. They also focused on her strengths, such as her good behavior and positive relationships at school. They explained that Tina's best chance to get help now was in juvenile court, where the focus would be on rehabilitation, not merely punishment, as in the adult system. But the adult court judge was still hesitant to send Tina to the juvenile court, where she would receive supervision for only three more years, until the age of 21. The judge told the defense team that he would not decertify Tina to juvenile court unless they came up with a program of services that would address Tina's mental health disorder, prepare her for the transition into adulthood, and satisfy his concerns.

The judge's assignment was a herculean task. Tina was almost too old for child services but too young for adult services. Her violent episode—combined with a Pennsylvania law that prohibited juveniles from being placed out of state—severely restricted the team's options in looking for an appropriate program for Tina. Some placements would not even consult with the legal team's social worker to review Tina's application and suitability for their program until Tina was actually transferred back to juvenile court—but the team needed to obtain conditional acceptances from programs to create a plan acceptable to the judge. Thanks in part to aggressive advocacy with service providers by the legal team's social worker, they presented the judge with a package of resources and services that would best meet Tina's current and future needs. The judge was persuaded and transferred Tina to juvenile court, where she pled guilty to aggravated assault.

But the legal team's work did not end with decertification. The next hurdle that the team faced was ensuring the right placement for Tina. The placement proposed by the defense team, though ideal for Tina's needs, required special funding from the local department of human services. At a hearing, the agency and the Medicaid managed care organization urged the judge to order Tina into a cheaper placement that they could pay for with Medicaid dollars. But the defense team knew the facility was ill equipped to help Tina, and presented evidence to that effect. Due in large part to the social worker's rigorous investigation into the range of placement options, and her knowledge of Tina's psychological profile and social history, the team convinced the judge to approve their proposed placement.

Tina was finally transferred to her new group home. But even then, the defense team's work did not end. Tina's new home was in another county, and she learned that it would be a few months before her health insurance transferred over. That meant that Tina did not have the financial means to fill her prescription for the psychotropic drugs that she needed to keep her bipolar disorder under control. Tina's legal defense team arranged for her doctor in Philadelphia to mail her a supply of medication while they sorted out her insurance.

At the group home, Tina receives mental health treatment and participates in services to prepare her for her upcoming transition to adulthood. Her defense team social worker regularly speaks with Tina and her counselors to monitor her progress in placement. The team troubleshoots and advocates for Tina as issues arise, because they know that Tina needs someone in her corner and her mother is not able to play that role. As her attorney explains, youth such as Tina often "have no one else."

## PART II: PREVENTING YOUTH FROM BEING TRIED AS ADULTS

During the 1980s and 1990s, most states made it easier to try juveniles in adult courts.[1] These legislative changes were prompted by an increase in media attention on juvenile crime, which also increased during the period and peaked in 1994. Even after juvenile crime started trending downward, public policy continued to shift toward prosecuting children in adult courts. Changes in law and policy broadened eligibility for youth to be tried as adults, shifting decision-making authority from judges to prosecutors, and reducing or eliminating discretion for judges and prosecutors.[2]

Consequently, most states have one or more mechanisms by which juveniles charged with offenses may be tried in adult criminal court. For example, in forty-five states, a juvenile court judge may waive juvenile court jurisdiction in certain juvenile cases, thus authorizing a transfer to criminal court. In addition, prosecutors in about fifteen states have the authority to file certain juvenile cases directly in criminal court. Finally, in certain states, statutes provide that cases meeting certain age and offense criteria are to be excluded from juvenile court jurisdiction and must be filed directly in criminal court.[3] But many states also have reverse waiver laws—such as

---

1. Kristin Johnson, Lonn Lanza-Kaduce & Jennifer Woolard, *Disregarding Graduated Treatment: Why Transfer Aggravates Recidivism*, 57 CRIME & DELINQUENCY 756, 757 (2011).

2. GRIFFIN ET AL., OFF. OF JUV. JUST. & DELINQUENCY PREVENTION, TRYING JUVENILES AS ADULTS: AN ANALYSIS OF STATE TRANSFER LAWS AND REPORTING 9 (2001).

3. CHARLES PUZZANCHERA, BENJAMIN ADAMS & SARAH HOCKENBERRY, OFF. OF JUV. JUST. & DELINQUENCY PREVENTION, JUVENILE COURT STATISTICS 2009 29 (2012); BENJAMIN

the Pennsylvania provision used in Tina's case—that allow youth whose cases are in adult criminal court to petition to have the case transferred, or "decertified," to the juvenile court.

It is difficult to determine how many youth are actually tried in adult court. It is estimated that approximately 250,000 youth each year become involved in the adult criminal justice system.[4] But no data source exists for nonwaiver cases—those in which juveniles are processed in criminal court as a result of statutory exclusions or prosecutors' discretionary choices.[5] Although there is scant data regarding nonwaiver cases, there is more data regarding cases transferred from juvenile court to adult court. In 2009, 7,600 cases in the United States were transferred from the juvenile court to the adult criminal court by judicial waiver, down from a high of 14,000 cases in 1994.[6] Much of the decline is associated with the concurrent decrease in violent crime.[7] However, part of the decline in judicial waivers can be ascribed to the simultaneous enactment of laws allowing direct filing in adult court, bypassing the juvenile court altogether.[8]

As in the juvenile justice system, youth of color are disproportionally represented in the adult criminal justice system. For much of the period from 1985 through 2009, the likelihood of judicial waiver for petitioned delinquency cases was greater for black youth than white youth for both offenses against persons and drug offense cases.[9] African American youth make up almost two-thirds of the youth in the adult criminal justice system and are nine times more likely than white youth to receive an adult prison sentence.[10]

ADAMS & SEAN ADDIE, NAT'L CTR. FOR JUV. JUST. & OFF. OF JUV. JUST. & DELINQUENCY PREVENTION, DELINQUENCY CASES WAIVED TO CRIMINAL COURT 2009 10, 40 (2012); GRIFFIN ET AL., *supra* note 2, at 5. *See also* JASON ZIEDENBERG, NAT'L INST. FOR CORR., YOU'RE AN ADULT NOW: YOUTH IN ADULT CRIMINAL JUSTICE SYSTEMS 3 (2011).

    4. ZIEDENBERG, *supra* note 3, at 3.

    5. GRIFFIN ET AL., *supra* note 2, at 12.

    6. PUZZANCHERA, ADAMS & HOCKENBERRY, *supra* note 3, at 29, 40, 58; CRYSTAL KNOLL & MELISSA SICKMUND, OFF. OF JUV. JUST. & DELINQUENCY PREVENTION, DELINQUENCY CASES IN JUVENILE COURT 2009 3 (2012).

    7. ADAMS & ADDIE, *supra* note 3, at 2.

    8. *Id.*; Johnson, Lanza-Kaduce & Woolard, *supra* note 1, at 757.

    9. ADAMS & ADDIE, *supra* note 3, at 4.

    10. ZIEDENBERG, *supra* note 3, at 7.

Unfortunately, trying juveniles in adult court continues to be a popular idea despite the fact that there is no empirical evidence to show that it is effective in reducing crime.[11] In fact, there is a growing body of research that shows that youth tried as adults recidivate at a higher rate than those who are kept in the juvenile courts.[12] Similarly, youth in the adult correctional system recidivate at a higher rate than youth in juvenile facilities.[13]

Public defender offices in some larger cities have organized specialized units to handle cases such as Tina's because they know what is at stake in keeping youth in juvenile court and out of the adult criminal system. (See Box 2, "Role of Juvenile Defense Counsel When Client Faces Risk of Adult Prosecution.") If tried and convicted as an adult, Tina would have faced a lengthy sentence. In juvenile court, she remained under court supervision until her twenty-first birthday. The adult criminal justice system does not have the same underlying mission of treatment and rehabilitation as the juvenile system. There are simply much fewer treatment options available.[14] In fact, the availability of more effective treatment in the juvenile system may be one reason why youth in adult criminal courts have higher recidivism rates.[15] On any given day, there are approximately 10,000 youth in adult prisons and jails,[16] where administrators struggle to keep them safe from physical and sexual abuse by other, older inmates, and to prevent them from committing suicide.[17]

Specialized units in public defender offices—such as the one that came to Tina's aid—use multidisciplinary teams to represent youth facing transfer to adult court. This is because courts typically consider a multitude of factors such as the youth's age and prior offense history, the seriousness of the offense, whether the child can be treated within the juvenile system while ensuring public safety, and whether the youth has exhausted all

---

11. GRIFFIN ET AL., *supra* note 2, at 26; Johnson, Lanza-Kaduce & Woolard, *supra* note 1, at 757.
12. Johnson, Lanza-Kaduce & Woolard, *supra* note 1, at 757, 760.
13. ZIEDENBERG, *supra* note 3, at 5.
14. Johnson, Lanza-Kaduce & Woolard, *supra* note 1, at 758.
15. *Id.* at 760.
16. ZIEDENBERG, *supra* note 3, at 6.
17. *Id.* at 11.

treatment options available within the juvenile justice system.[18] Lawyers need the help of social workers and other professionals to give courts the evidence they need to keep kids in juvenile court. (See Box 1, "Checklist for Reviewing Expert Evaluations.") In Tina's case, the team emphasized that Tina's recent bipolar diagnosis, as well as her untreated history of trauma, could be effectively treated in the juvenile court system, but would likely never be addressed if Tina ended up in an adult prison. Tina's mental health issues are not unique in juvenile court. Empirical studies suggest that 65%–75% of youth involved in the justice system have one or more diagnosable psychiatric disorders, including major depression and mood, anxiety, and substance use disorders.[19] Additionally, the majority of youth in the juvenile justice system have experienced trauma, having been exposed to community and family violence and/or been threatened with, or been the direct target of, such violence.[20] The team's investigation of Tina's social background also was critical, as it showed that Tina's aggressive behavior was limited to her toxic relationship with her mother, and that she had generally good behavior in structured settings such as school. The team's knowledge of her social history and mental health needs also helped in the battle with bureaucracies, when the team had to fight for the best placement for Tina, not the cheapest. (See Box 3, "Preparing for Disposition.")

As Tina's case demonstrates, lawyers for youth also play an important role in postdisposition advocacy. Lawyers and the professionals with whom they collaborate ensure that youth are receiving all court-ordered treatment,

---

18. Johnson, Lanza-Kaduce & Woolard, *supra* note 1, at 758.

19. JENNIE L. SHUFELT & JOSEPH J. COCOZZA, NAT'L CTR. FOR MENTAL HEALTH & JUV. JUST., YOUTH WITH MENTAL HEATLH DISORDERS IN THE JUVENILE JUSTICE SYSTEM: RESULTS FROM A MULTI-STATE PREVALENCE STUDY 2 (2006); Linda A. Teplin, Karen M. Abram, Gary M. McClennan, Mina K. Dulcan & Amy A. Mericle, *Psychiatric Disorders in the Juvenile Justice System*, 59 ARCHIVES GEN. PSYCHIATRY 1111, 1133–43 (2002); Gail A. Wasserman, Larkin S. McReynolds, Susan J. Ko, Laura M. Katz & Jennifer R. Carpenter, *Gender Differences in Psychiatric Disorders at Juvenile Probation Intake*, 95 AM. J. PUB. HEALTH 131, 133–34 (2005); Gail A. Wasserman, Larkin S. McReynolds, Christopher P. Lucas, Prudence Fisher & Linda Santos, *The Voice DISC-IV with Incarcerated Male Youth: Prevalence of Disorder*, 41 J. AM. ACAD. CHILD & ADOLESCENT PSYCHIATRY 314, 317 (2002).

20. KRISTINE BUFFINGTON, CARLY B. DIERKHISING & SHAWN C. MARSH, NAT'L COUNCIL OF JUV. & FAM. CT. JUDGES, TEN THINGS EVERY JUVENILE COURT JUDGE SHOULD KNOW ABOUT TRAUMA AND DELINQUENCY 2, 6 (2010).

education, and services. Legal teams also play an important role in acting as unofficial monitors or watchdogs of placement facilities and can report back to the courts and contracting agencies about the quality of the programming and any safety concerns.

Finally, Tina's case illustrates well that youth in the justice system are not "mini-adults." As the new information we have learned about adolescent brain development indicates, juveniles are at a unique developmental stage that must be taken into account at all phases of their court cases. Since 2005, the United States Supreme Court has issued four major opinions that have reaffirmed the principle that youth are developmentally different than adults in ways that matter when they become involved with the justice system.[21] In particular, these cases recognize what any parent of a teenager will tell you: adolescents lack maturity and have an underdeveloped sense of responsibility; they are vulnerable to negative influences and outside pressures; their characters are transient and developing; they have limited ability to control their immediate circumstances and environments; and for all these reasons, they are less culpable than adults.[22] The holdings of these key United States Supreme Court cases have set the stage for even more zealous advocacy on behalf of youth facing prosecution as adults, as well as systemic reform of how the justice system treats children and adolescents.

---

21. The four cases are as follows: Roper v. Simmons, 543 U.S. 551, 578 (2005) (holding that imposing the death penalty on individuals who committed murders as juveniles violated the Eighth Amendment's prohibition against cruel and unusual punishment); Graham v. Florida, 130 S. Ct. 2011, 2034 (2010) (holding that it is unconstitutional to impose life without parole sentences on juveniles convicted of nonhomicide offenses); J.D.B. v. North Carolina, 131 S. Ct. 2394, 2403 (2011) (holding that a child's age must be taken into account for the purposes of the *Miranda* custody test); and Miller v. Alabama, 132 S. Ct. 2455 (2012) (holding that mandatory life without parole sentence for juveniles is unconstitutional).

22. *Roper*, 543 U.S. at 569–71; *Miller*, 132 S. Ct. at 2464–65.

## Box 1: Checklist for Reviewing Expert Evaluations

- Is the correct legal issue addressed?
- Did the expert identify sources of information?
- Are any important information sources missing?
- Did the expert note how much time was spent with the examinee?
- Did the expert consider the juvenile's behavior from a developmental and situational perspective?
- Is there a rich description of the examinee and the legally relevant behaviors?
- Is there a clear relationship between any opinions offered and the data underlying them?
- Has the expert made his or her reasoning clear?
- Did the expert consider and appropriately rule out alternative explanations or conceptualizations?
- Does the report comport with the relevant statutes and court rules?
- Were the tests used appropriate, especially taking into consideration the examinee's age, sex, and ethnicity?
- Does the evaluation enhance your ability to defend your client?

JUVENILE DEFENDER DELINQUENCY NOTEBOOK 56 (Elizabeth Calvin, Sarah Marcus, George Oleyer & Mary Ann Scali eds., 2d ed. 2006).

## Box 2: Role of Juvenile Defense Counsel When Client Faces Risk of Adult Prosecution

The National Juvenile Defender Center has issued the following standards for the representation of juveniles who are at risk of prosecution in adult criminal court:

8.1 Specialized Training and Experience Necessary

Specialized training and experience are prerequisites to providing

*Continued*

**99**

## Box 2: Role of Juvenile Defense Counsel When Client Faces Risk of Adult Prosecution *Continued*

effective assistance of counsel to youth facing adult prosecution.

a. Counsel must be familiar with relevant statutes and case law regarding the interplay between adult and juvenile prosecution, including presumptions in favor of or against keeping youth in juvenile court and the burden of proof necessary to overcome such a presumption. Counsel must be aware of the timing and process of transfer hearings and required findings for transfer of jurisdiction to adult court. In jurisdictions in which the attorney handling the transfer hearing will also represent the client at any criminal court proceedings, counsel must be aware of adult criminal court rules, sentencing guidelines, and rules of evidence;

b. Counsel must also be knowledgeable and aware of the extent to which adult facilities provide young clients legally mandated safety protections, medical and mental health care, rehabilitative treatment, and mandatory education services to which they are entitled;

c. Counsel must pursue specialized training, including in the areas of child and adolescent development, to ensure the requisite level of knowledge and skill to represent a youth in a transfer hearing or in adult court, and be familiar with developmental issues that may affect competence to stand trial; and

d. When the youth will be tried in adult court, counsel has the responsibility of educating the adult court stakeholders, including new defense counsel if applicable, of the special developmental considerations of youth. Counsel must use child development research and case law supporting the lessened culpability of adolescent offenders in arguing intent, capacity, and the appropriateness of rehabilitative sentencing options.

8.2 Inform the Client of the Nature of Transfer Proceedings and Potential Consequences

Counsel must use developmentally appropriate language to fully

**100**

advise the client of the procedures that may lead to adult prosecution and the various ways that the state could proceed.

    a. Counsel must be well-versed in the procedures that could lead to adult prosecution, as well as the consequences of adult prosecution; and

    b. Counsel must explain the consequences of prosecution in adult court, including the extent of possible sentencing decisions, as well as collateral consequences. Counsel must advise which venue would be most likely to achieve the client's expressed interest.

8.3 Conduct Investigation for Clients Facing Adult Prosecution

Counsel must conduct timely and thorough investigation of the circumstances of the allegations and the client's background in any case where the client may be prosecuted in adult court.

    a. Counsel must understand what factors weigh for and against transfer to adult court and must investigate the case accordingly;

    b. Counsel must quickly compile and coordinate all evidence and information bearing on the transfer decision, including case law and research regarding adolescent development, and develop cogent arguments that support the client's expressed interests; and

    c. Counsel must advocate for the client's expressed interests regarding jurisdiction with prosecutors and other stakeholders in advance of a transfer proceeding or in cases when direct file to adult court might be an option.

8.4 Advocate Against Transfer of Client to Adult Court

Counsel must, when in the client's expressed interests, endeavor to prevent adult prosecution of the client.

    a. Counsel's pleadings during the stages that determine the court of jurisdiction must specify with particularity the grounds for opposing adult prosecution, including, but not limited to: the sufficiency of the offense to warrant adult prosecution; the prosecutor's failure to establish probable cause; the client's amenability

*Continued*

**101**

## Box 2: Role of Juvenile Defense Counsel When Client Faces Risk of Adult Prosecution *Continued*

to rehabilitation in the juvenile system; the client's incompetence to proceed in adult court; and other applicable state-specific statutory criteria;

b. To preserve the client's right to appeal, counsel must ensure that any jurisdiction-related hearing is on the record;

c. When a prosecutor could elect to file charges that lead to adult prosecution, counsel must present all facts and mitigating evidence to dissuade the prosecutor. If the prosecutor ultimately files charges that could lead to adult prosecution, counsel must insist on a hearing (whether that be a transfer hearing, reverse-waiver hearing, or some other jurisdictionally appropriate mechanism) to prevent prosecution in adult court as a matter of the client's right to due process;

d. Counsel must seek to obtain and review any report developed by probation prior to the hearing; and

e. At the hearing, counsel must:

1. Challenge any defect in the charges that would deprive the adult court of jurisdiction;

2. Raise any credible facial or "as applied" state or federal constitutional challenges to adult prosecution;

3. Present all facts, mitigating evidence, and testimony that may convince the court to keep the client in juvenile court, including the client's amenability to treatment and the availability of tailored treatment options in juvenile court; and

4. Consider use of expert witnesses to raise the client's capacity to proceed in adult court, amenability to rehabilitation in juvenile court, and related developmental issues.

8.5 Preserve Client's Opportunity to Appeal a Judicial Decision to Prosecute in Adult Court

Counsel must adequately preserve the record for appeal. Counsel must apprise the client, in a timely manner and using developmentally appropriate language, of the opportunity and procedures to appeal a judicial decision to prosecute the client in adult court.

a. Counsel must adhere to statutory requirements for the timing and/or perfecting of the appeal of the judicial decision to prosecute the client in adult court. When appropriate, counsel should move for interlocutory appeal of the judicial decision in a timely manner to reduce the length of time a detained client spends incarcerated and to avoid the removal of the client to an adult jail; and

b. Counsel should insist that the court make findings of fact and law on the record and should obtain copies of any orders detailing how the court's decisions meet the statutory requirements for adult prosecution.

8.6 Obligations Following a Determination to Prosecute the Client in Adult Court

Upon determination that the client will be prosecuted in adult court, counsel must zealously oppose placement of the client in adult jail or detention. Counsel must be aware of and raise the risks associated with incarcerating young people among adults, and be able to propose alternative placements in the juvenile justice system and/or release of the client on bail. If the case is transferred to adult court and the client is assigned a different lawyer, counsel should work closely with the new attorney to ensure a smooth transition of the case.

NAT'L JUV. DEFENDER CTR., NATIONAL JUVENILE DEFENSE STANDARDS, pt. VIII (2012).

## Box 3: Preparing for Disposition

1. Counsel and confer with your client.
   a. Advise your client of all the possible dispositions that the court

*Continued*

**103**

## Box 3: Preparing for Disposition *Continued*

may order and what is realistic for your client to expect.

    b.   Counsel your client about upcoming interviews with probation officers, court personnel, clinicians, and others who have been charged with preparing disposition reports for the court.

    c.   Seek your client's preferences about the desired dispositions and begin preparing to present a plan to the court to accomplish your client's desired result.

2.   Discuss the disposition process with your client's parent/guardian. (But remember, this may not be possible when there is conflict between the parent's and client's position. When such a conflict arises, the attorney's ethical obligation is to the child client.)

    a.   Advise your client's parent/guardian of all the possible dispositions that the court may order and what is realistic to expect.

    b.   Counsel your client's parent/guardian about upcoming interviews with probation officers, court personnel, clinicians, and others who have been charged with preparing disposition reports for the court.

    c.   Determine the disposition preference of your client's parent/guardian. Assess whether the preference of the parent/guardian is consistent with or opposed to your client's preference. If the parent/guardian's preference is opposed to your client's desired result—for example, the parent/guardian refuses to have the youth come home at this time and the youth wants to be placed on probation while living in the parent/guardian's home—you will need to consult further with your client and come up with an alternative disposition plan.

3.   Meet with probation officers, court personnel, clinicians, and others who are preparing disposition reports *before* they finalize their reports and submit them to the court. Provide these individuals with information about your client, including correcting any incorrect information they may have heard, and advocate for your client's desired disposition.

4. Obtain and review all copies of any disposition reports and evaluations, as well as the records that the preparers relied on, in advance of the disposition hearing. If necessary, begin preparing for an evidentiary hearing at the disposition hearing to challenge the findings of the reports and present your own evidence.

5. Meet with probation officers, court personnel, clinicians, and others again *after* they finalize their reports and submit them to the court. If the reports contain unfavorable recommendations, provide these individuals with information about events since the writing of the report that may influence them to change their recommendations. This is also an opportunity for you to begin thinking about how you can refute the bases underlying the unfavorable recommendations.

6. Secure your own evaluations of your client to present at disposition. These can include mental health, special education, and developmental disabilities evaluations.

7. Engage a social worker on behalf of your client to assist you with disposition planning and to testify at the disposition hearing. "Often the most important resource for the respondent in developing a dispositional alternative that the court is likely to accept is a trained and knowledgeable social worker."[23] Ideally, you will want to retain a social worker with extensive knowledge of programs and services available to your client. The social worker can also assist you in analyzing and challenging the findings and conclusions in the various reports and evaluations that the court will consider, and in obtaining your own evaluations for your client.

8. Find suitable community-based or residential programs for your client as an alternative to incarceration and arrange for your client's admission into the programs before the disposition hearing.

9. Gather mitigating evidence and letters of support for your client.

10. Negotiate with the probation officer, other court personnel, and the prosecutor to, if possible, come to agreement on a disposition

*Continued*

---

23. *Id.* at 701.

## Box 3: Preparing for Disposition *Continued*

plan to submit to the court.

11. Prepare and submit a disposition memorandum to the court, including information about the programs to which your client has been admitted.

Adapted from RANDY HERTZ, MARTIN GUGGENHEIM, & ANTHONY G. AMSTERDAM, NATIONAL JUVENILE DEFENDER CENTER, TRIAL MANUAL FOR DEFENSE ATTORNEYS IN JUVENILE DELINQUENCY CASES, §§ 38.05–17 (2012).

# CHAPTER EIGHT

## Keeping the Door Open
# Representing Older Youth Transitioning Out of Foster Care

By Franchesca L. Hamilton-Acker

### PART I: CALEB'S STORY

When 16-year-old Caleb appeared in a court in a rural town in Louisiana to answer to a charge of unauthorized use of a vehicle, the judge quickly saw that there was a much more urgent matter to address. Observing a visibly shaken Caleb covered in bandages, the judge questioned Caleb about his injuries and how they had been caused. Caleb told the judge that the injuries had been inflicted by his mother. The judge became less interested in the delinquency proceeding when he learned that Caleb could be a victim of abuse. The judge immediately ordered the Department of Children and Family Services to take Caleb into state's custody and to investigate further.

Caleb was appointed an attorney by the judge to represent him as the child victim in the Child in Need of Care case pursuant to Louisiana law. When the attorney met with Caleb for the first time, Caleb was confused and scared. He had never been in any trouble with the law before. Although he answered the lawyer's questions in a respectful manner, Caleb's responses were limited. The attorney saw that Caleb was very hesitant to volunteer information about his home life, including the details about his injuries. So she explained to Caleb her role and obligations as Caleb's attorney, including that she would not disclose any information he provided to her unless he gave her permission to do so. Once Caleb understood this, he opened up much more to his attorney.

Caleb and his attorney next appeared at a continued custody hearing in his Child in Need of Care case. The same district attorney handling Caleb's delinquency case represented the state. At the continued custody hearing, the district attorney moved to dismiss the order placing Caleb into state care and for the court to release Caleb back into his parents' custody. The district attorney—failing to differentiate his role as a prosecutor in a delinquency proceeding from his role in representing the state in its obligation in a Child in Need of Care proceeding—attempted to portray Caleb as a defiant, troubled, and unruly youth. Hearing all this, Caleb became extremely nervous and agitated. He cried, his hands shook, and he could not stop tapping his toes and fidgeting. It was at this point that Caleb's attorney advised him that he could speak directly to the judge in chambers without anyone but his attorney present. When Caleb told her that was what he wanted, the attorney made this request. The attorneys for Caleb's mother and father objected, arguing their clients should be able to hear the testimony against them. Caleb's attorney countered that Caleb was obviously traumatized by this process and being in the presence of his mother, who had inflicted significant harm upon him, and was unable to effectively express himself accordingly in her presence. The judge agreed to speak with Caleb alone.

One-on-one with the judge and with his attorney at his side, Caleb was empowered to speak freely. The judge asked Caleb if he felt safe at home. Caleb said that he felt a little safer when his father was home. (Caleb's father worked offshore and was home on a limited basis.) Caleb said that he did not feel safe when he was alone with his mother. Caleb explained to the judge that he was covered in bandages because his mother hit him with a black cast iron skillet the day before the vehicle incident that gave rise to the pending delinquency charge. Caleb explained that his mother became very upset with him, claiming that he had not done the dishes, and attacked him with the skillet. But Caleb had washed the dishes; his mother subsequently used a dish and put it in the sink, and used this excuse to come after Caleb. Caleb had a 19-year-old brother who still lived at home, and a 12-year-old sister. Caleb's mother would often become physically violent with him and his siblings for no reason. But Caleb was his mother's most favored target.

Caleb also told the judge that the alleged unauthorized vehicle he had been driving belonged to his brother. His brother and mother had both given him permission to drive his brother's car to visit a friend. But when Caleb did not return on time, his mother convinced Caleb's brother to call the police and report his car as stolen. Having never been in trouble before, Caleb was very concerned about being cleared on those charges.

After talking with Caleb, the judge then proceeded with a full hearing on the record, in which his attorney marshaled evidence to demonstrate that Caleb was indeed a child in need of the state's care. The evidence offered by Caleb's attorney included certified medical records from numerous emergency room visits. Although Caleb did not testify at this hearing, relevant and favorable evidence to Caleb's case was obtained through effective cross-examination of Caleb's mother and father. The undisputed evidence established during the hearing that Caleb and his siblings were all born of the marriage of their Caucasian mother and African American father. None of the children had ever attended a traditional school; all were home schooled by the mother. The children's chores would take up to five hours daily, and they never participated in any recreational activities. Caleb went to the emergency room multiple times over the years, starting at age five. The medical records noted peculiar reasons for the injuries, such as that Caleb tripped on a rake while working in the yard. After two full days of testimony, the judge found that Caleb was a child in need of care and ordered that Caleb remain in state custody.

The Department of Children and Family Services (DCFS) was initially very resistant to working with Caleb because he entered foster care through the juvenile justice system. In the months that followed, Caleb's attorney had to fight vigorously to ensure that the state found an appropriate placement for him. At first, Caleb was placed in a juvenile detention home. DCFS maintained that it did not have any other placements suitable for someone Caleb's age with a delinquency charge. Caleb's attorney quickly motioned the court to order a change of placement, successfully arguing that the detention home was contrary to Caleb's welfare. Louisiana law supports that a judge can make a determination that a placement does not serve the best interest and welfare of a child and order a change of placement. However, the judge may not order a specific placement for a child in state custody, and instead must rely on DCFS to find a suitable home for the child.

DCFS next moved Caleb to a children's shelter 30 miles away. Although Caleb was technically considered to be age appropriate for this placement, the placement catered more to younger children. In addition, this shelter was an emergency placement option that was limited to a 45-day stay, and it was becoming apparent Caleb would need more than a temporary placement. Both Caleb's mother and father were unwilling to cooperate with DCFS services, making it likely that Caleb would remain in state custody until he aged out of foster care. While Caleb was disappointed about being abandoned by his parents, he was also concerned about losing touch with his siblings, with whom he had a close bond. While he could visit with his older brother, who was an adult and could see Caleb outside their parents' home, Caleb's parents were not allowing Caleb to visit with his sister. Moreover, DCFS had made no arrangements for Caleb's education in the month since the continued custody hearing despite repeated follow-up by his attorney. Caleb had been told by his mother that he had completed his secondary educational requirements and that they were awaiting his certificate. DCFS told the attorney that Caleb's mother refused to provide a signed authorization so that DCFS could obtain his records from the home schooling program (located out of state) that Caleb's mother utilized. Caleb's attorney once again motioned the court to resolve these issues. With regard to placement, DCFS testified that no other certified placements were available for Caleb at that time. But the judge did not accept this and ordered DCFS to find another placement for Caleb. Moreover, he ordered DCFS to obtain Caleb's education records and to enroll him in an educational program pending receipt of his records. He also ordered that Caleb have phone contact with his sister and that DCFS facilitate in-person visits.

DCFS subsequently moved Caleb from the children's shelter to a placement 120 miles away from his home parish. Caleb was placed in an independent living program in a more metropolitan area, but it was difficult for him to adjust because he did not have the confidence or the daily living skills that youth in the program were expected to have. Moreover, Caleb contacted his attorney after a week in his new placement to inform her that he had been attacked by his roommate. Caleb said the new placement was scary. Caleb tried to contact the staff person on duty to report the attack but did not get an immediate response. (The means of communicating with the staff on duty was by phone.) When Caleb didn't get a response from staff, he called 911. An ambulance responded and transported Caleb to the hospital, where he was treated for a head injury.

Immediately following this unfortunate event, Caleb's attorney filed an emergency motion to get Caleb's case back into court to challenge his placement and to get an update on the education issues. Caleb's attorney informed the judge that Caleb was housed with youth in Office of Juvenile Justice (OJJ) custody who had been adjudicated delinquent, as well as homeless youth, and that Caleb had been assaulted. Perturbed by this information, the judge challenged DCFS to provide a rationale for this latest inappropriate placement. DCFS again argued that this was the only placement available for Caleb at that time, a claim that was quickly belied by evidence submitted by Caleb's attorney. Through her independent research, she identified Goodwill Industries Transitioning Youth Home as an appropriate placement option for Caleb. The program provided an independent living arrangement for young men transitioning out of state custody, and was independently funded by, and an approved provider of, the Department of Social Services. Caleb's attorney had described the program to Caleb before the hearing, and Caleb was in agreement that he should go there. The DCFS representatives in court, however, instantly rejected this option without providing a sound reason to the judge. Determined to get to the bottom of the placement challenges for Caleb, the judge recessed court to consult with the DCFS placement agent by phone. The DCFS placement agent advised the judge that there was no space available in the program. Anticipating such a roadblock, Caleb's attorney had arranged for the executive director for Goodwill Industries, who oversaw the Youth Transitional Home, to be on standby to speak to the judge. The judge immediately called the executive director, who verified that there was space in their program and that they would like to accept Caleb as a client. The court ordered DCFS to move him from the facility 120 miles away. The judge strongly urged that the Goodwill Industries placement be explored. At this same hearing, DCFS reported that Caleb had only completed fifth grade. Contrary to what his mother had told him, Caleb was severely deficient in his educational progress. The court ordered that DCFS develop a plan to address Caleb's educational needs to be submitted to the court for approval.

Caleb was moved back to the emergency children's shelter until a placement could be confirmed for Caleb. Meanwhile, Goodwill Industries continued to hold Caleb's position. Subsequently, at a meeting between DCFS, the Goodwill Industries executive director, and Caleb's attorney, the parties concluded that Caleb would be moved to the Goodwill Transitional Youth Program.

Once Caleb entered the Goodwill Transitional Youth Program, he began to work on his GED and received regular counseling. Caleb benefited greatly from the Goodwill Transitional Youth Program by learning essential life skills. He learned how to maintain his personal living space, effectively budget, be attentive to his personal needs, and live harmoniously with other youth in a communal living environment. Caleb remained in that placement until he turned 18. Upon turning 18, Caleb benefited from Louisiana's Young Adult Program, a transition program that provides for benefits such as a subsidy for housing for youth such as Caleb who age out of foster care. Today, Caleb lives independently, works full time, and attends a technical college. He continues to be estranged from his parents but has a relationship with his siblings.

## PART II: THE FOSTER CARE SYSTEM FOR TRANSITIONING FOSTER YOUTH

Foster care is a system in which government authorities assume temporary responsibility for minors who have been removed from their primary caretakers (birth parents or other custodial adults) due to a risk of abuse, neglect, and/or other relevant reasons.[1] The age demographic of foster care children has been changing over the past several years, with an increasing percentage of foster youth nationwide "aging out" of care upon reaching

---

1. Lisa Han, Vivian Hsu & Derek Ishikawa, UCLA SCH. OF PUB. AFF., PUB. POL'Y DEP'T, AGING OUT: IMPROVING OUTCOMES FOR OLDER FOSTER CARE YOUTH 1 (2009).

their state's legal age of majority.[2] "Aging out" is a term used to describe foster youth who leave court and child welfare jurisdiction, commonly at age 18, after the foster care system has failed in the goal of either reunifying a child with his or her biological family or finding an alternative permanent placement for the youth.[3]

Although the foster care system is designed to promote reunification of youth with their primary caretakers, this option is often unavailable. Achieving permanency is a challenge for all foster youth, but especially so for older youth in foster care.[4] Like many other older foster youth, Caleb did not have the opportunity to live with a foster family; it is difficult to recruit foster families to take older youth, and child welfare agencies often do not aggressively seek out such foster families despite the federal mandate to secure the most family-like setting in which to place all foster children. While great strides are being made in achieving permanency for younger foster children, there is a growing concern about the outcomes of these older youth who leave the system unprepared and without the necessary social supports to succeed as independent adults.[5]

Caleb was different from the typical child who enters the foster care system in two ways: he was older and entered by way of the juvenile justice system.[6] But the rest of his experience within the foster care system was not far removed from that of other children. Most foster youth, including older youth, confront the challenges of living in multiple placements, trying

---

2. *See* U.S. Dep't of Health & Hum. Serv. Admin. for Child. & Fam., Child. Bureau, *Adoption and Foster Care Analysis and Reporting System (AFCARS) Reports* #10, #11, #12, #13, #14 (2003–2006), *available at* http://www.acf.hhs.gov/programs/cb/research-data-technology /statistics-research/afcars.

3. Han, Hsu & Ishikawa, *supra* note 1, at 2.

4. *Id.*

5. *See* U.S. Dep't of Health & Hum. Serv. Admin. for Child. & Fam., Child. Bureau, *Adoption and Foster Care Analysis and Reporting System (AFCARS) Reports* #10, #11, #12, #13, #14 (2003–2006), *available at* http://www.acf.hhs.gov/programs/cb/research-data-technology /statistics-research/afcars.

6. In one other respect, Caleb was representative of others in the child welfare system. Children of color are disproportionately represented in the United States foster care system. *See* National Council of Juvenile and Family Court Judges, *Disproportionality Rates of Children of Color in Foster Care* (May 2013), available at http://www.ncjfcj.org/sites/default/ files/Disproportionality%20Rates%20for%20Children%20of%20Color%20in%20Foster %20Care%202013.pdf.

to pursue an education and obtain the appropriate services, and maintaining familial bonds. Approximately 26,000 children "age out" of foster care each year, and many of these children will not have a permanent home.[7]

Being placed in foster care is traumatic for children and, unfortunately, many "graduates" of the system experience poor outcomes, including poverty, homelessness, and involvement with the criminal justice system.[8] Older foster youth are failing to triumph over the many obstacles to attaining a postsecondary education, employment, and housing stability, and to staying out of the criminal justice system and off of public assistance. According to a 2011 Chapin Hall report that tracked outcomes of young adults (ages 23–24) who once were in foster care, nearly one-quarter did not have a high school diploma or GED.[9] Fewer than one-half were currently employed,[10] and the median income for those who had been employed was only $8,000 per year.[11] More than one-quarter had no income during the past year.[12] Almost one-half had experienced material economic hardships such as not having enough money to pay rent or having utilities disconnected.[13] Nearly one-half had either been homeless or "couch surfed" since leaving foster care.[14] More than two-thirds of the women had been pregnant since leaving foster care, and two-thirds of those who had ever been pregnant had been pregnant more than once.[15] Forty-five percent of young men in the group had been incarcerated.[16] The average older youth aging out of foster care faces these odds with minimal resources in place to assist in defeating them.

---

7. Han, Hsu & Ishikawa, *supra* note 1, at 2. These numbers—provided by the U.S. Department of Health and Human Services—are from 2006. *Id.*

8. *See, e.g.*, Joseph Doyle Jr., *Child Protection and Adult Crime: Using Investigator Assignment to Estimate Causal Effects of Foster Care*, 116 (4) J. POL. ECON. 746 (2008).

9. MARK E. COURTNEY, AMY DWORSKY, JOANN S. LEE & MELISSA RAAP, CHAPIN HALL AT THE UNIV. OF CHICAGO, MIDWEST EVALUATION OF THE ADULT FUNCTIONING OF FORMER FOSTER YOUTH: OUTCOMES AT AGE 23 AND 24, at 22 (2011).

10. *Id.* at 27.

11. *Id.* at 32.

12. *Id.*

13. *Id.* at 35.

14. *Id.* at 10.

15. *Id.* at 49.

16. *Id.* at 67.

Several federal initiatives over the last decade—including the John H. Chafee Foster Care Independence Program established in Title I of the Foster Care Independence Act ("Chafee Program"),[17] the Fostering Connections to Success and Increasing Adoptions Act of 2008 ("Fostering Connections"),[18] and the Affordable Care Act[19]—provide critical resources and protections for older youth in the child welfare system as well as former foster youth who are now young adults. For example, federal law requires child welfare agencies to develop case plans for youth in their care, which for a child age 16 years or older must include a written description of the programs and services that will help such child prepare for the transition from foster care to independent living,[20] as well as plan for educational stability.[21] At review hearings, courts must find that children 16 and older in state care are receiving the services needed to assist the child to make the transition from foster care to independent living.[22] Under federal law, states now have the option to extend foster care, guardianship, and adoption subsidies until age 21 for permanency arrangements entered into when a youth in care was 16 years of age or older.[23] Attorneys who represent foster children in states that currently do not offer this option are vigorously advocating for their legislatures to enact legislation to allow youth

---

17. Foster Care Independence Act of 1999, Pub. L. No. 106-169, 113 Stat. 1822 (1999).

18. Fostering Connections to Success and Increasing Adoption Act of 2008, Pub. L. No. 110-351, 122 Stat. 3949 (2008).

19. Affordable Care Act of 2010, Pub. L. No. 111-148, 124 Stat. 119 (2010).

20. 42 U.S.C.A. § 675(1)(D) (2011).

21. 42 U.S.C.A. § 675(1)(G) (2011).

22. 42 U.S.C.A. § 675(5)(C)(i) (2011).

23. 42 U.S.C.A. § 675(8)(B) (2011). Under this provision, states' child welfare systems have the option to expand the definition of a child to include an individual who is under the age of 21 and meets any of the following criteria:

is completing secondary education or a program leading to an equivalent credential;
is enrolled in an institution that provides postsecondary or vocational education;
is participating in a program or activity designed to promote, or remove barriers to, employment;
is employed for at least eighty hours per month; or
is incapable of engaging in any of the above activities due to a medical condition, which incapability is supported by regularly updated information in the case plan of the child.

*Id.*

to stay in care until age 21. States also may seek Title IV-E reimbursement for "a supervised setting in which the individual is living independently..." for youth ages 18–21.[24]

Nor does the state's legal obligation end when the youth is ready to leave its care. Federal law requires child welfare agencies to develop a transition plan during the ninety-day period prior to discharging a youth from state care or ending after care services for a youth age 18 or older who already has left care.[25] The transition plan should include specific details about the youth's housing, health insurance, education, local opportunities for mentors and continuing support services, and work force supports and employment services for when the youth has left care.[26] (See Box 2, "Checklist for Developing a Transition Plan with Your Youth Client.) The Chafee Program requires states to certify that they will provide "assistance and services to children who have left foster care because they have attained 18 years of age, and who have not attained 21 years of age."[27] The Chafee Program also offers Education and Training Vouchers (ETVs) of up to $5,000 per year for eligible youth to attend postsecondary education and vocational programs; eligible youth include those who were in foster care placement on or after their 14th birthday, and youth adopted from foster care or placed in a relative guardianship from foster care after reaching age 16.[28] And under the Affordable Care Act, starting in 2014, states must provide Medicaid to former foster youth up until the age of 26.[29] These are important tools for the attorney to wield on behalf of his/her clients.

---

24. 42 U.S.C.A. § 672(c)(2) (2010). Federal guidance provides states great flexibility in designing this option. Examples can include dormitories, apartments, host homes, and direct payments to youth to fund housing. See program instructions at http://www.acf.hhs.gov/programs/cb/resource/pi1011.

25. 42 U.S.C.A. § 675(5)(H) (2011).

26. *Id.*

27. 42 U.S.C.A. § 677(b)(3)(A) (2010).

28. 42 U.S.C.A. § 677(a)(7), 677(i)(2) (2010).

29. *See* Ctr. for the Stud. of Soc. Pol'y, *The Affordable Care Act & Implications for Youth Aging Out of Foster Care, available at* http://www.cssp.org/policy/2013/The-Affordable-Care-Act-and-Implications-for-Youth-Aging-Out-of-Foster-Care.pdf. *See also* Appeal Processes Related to Eligibility and Enrollment for Medicaid and CHIP, 78 Fed. Reg. 4593-4724 (proposed Jan. 22, 2013).

Caleb had an attorney who represented his voice to an attentive dependency court judge, neither of whom would accept the status quo as being sufficient to ensure Caleb's safety and well-being. Positive outcomes for youth in dependency cases often hinge on the child being represented by an experienced attorney who fulfills the duties of loyalty and confidentiality to the child. Accordingly, the ABA Model Act Governing the Representation of Children in Abuse, Neglect, and Dependency Proceedings provides that when a youth is capable of directing the representation by expressing his or her objectives, the child's attorney shall maintain a normal attorney-client relationship with the child in accordance with the rules of professional conduct.[30] (See Box 1, "Advocating for the Transitioning Youth: A Checklist for Attorneys.") Additionally, studies have focused on the important role that the court can play in improving outcomes for foster youth of all ages, but especially for those youth who will age out of the system.[31] Dependency judges with longer terms are more likely to gain the experience and knowledge with child welfare issues as compared to judges who quickly rotate off of dependency cases after short terms.[32] As Caleb's case well demonstrates, committed and experienced attorneys and judges are critical to promoting better outcomes for all foster youth.

## Box 1: Advocating for the Transitioning Youth: A Checklist for Attorneys

1. Is the youth engaged in his/her case?
2. Does the youth have access to his/her attorney? Is the youth actively engaged in the direction of his case? Is the youth attending court?
3. Has the youth been consulted about permanency planning? Has the youth been asked to identify permanency resources? Has a

*Continued*

---

30. ABA Model Act Governing the Representation of Children in Abuse, Neglect, and Dependency Proceedings (2011). The standards were formally adopted by the ABA House of Delegates in August 2011. The Model Act is available at http://apps.americanbar.org/litigation/committees/childrights/docs/aba_model_act_2011.pdf.

31. HAN, HSU & ISHIKAWA, *supra* note 1, at 29.

32. *Id.* at 30.

## Box 1: Advocating for the Transitioning Youth: A Checklist for Attorneys *Continued*

permanency plan been reached?

4. Is the youth actively participating in his/her case planning? Is the youth 12 or older attending the family team meetings and providing input about his/her case plan?

5. Are the case plan objectives attainable? What services are being provided to meet these objectives?

6. What is the status of placement/current posture?

   a. How many placements has the youth been in since the last review hearing?

   b. Is this the least restrictive, most familylike environment? Have reasonable efforts been taken to move the youth from a congregate care setting to a more familylike setting?

   c. How does the placement help the youth achieve the identified permanency plan?

   d. Is the youth a teen parent? If yes, has a plan been developed to include the care of the youth's child?

7. What is the youth's independent living plan?

   a. Has the youth been referred to an independent living program? If not, how are the youth's independent living needs being met?

   b. What services are being provided to meet the youth's independent living/transition needs? Are accommodations being provided for any disabilities or special challenges?

8. What is the youth's educational status?

   a. Is the youth currently enrolled in school?

   b. What is the youth's educational aspiration?

   c. If the youth receives special education services, when was the last IEP meeting?

   d. Has the youth received services to prepare him or her for post-secondary education or training if applicable?

9. What health and medical coverage does the youth have?

   a. Is the youth up to date on all medical care?

    b.   List any special health care needs and how they are being addressed. Provide any behavioral health referrals or assessments.

    c.   Has the youth been provided with information regarding family planning services?

    d.   If the youth has behavioral health needs, what services are being provided to address these needs?

    e.   What plans are in place to ensure continuity of treatment for health (including mental health) needs?

    f.   If the youth has drug and alcohol abuse needs, what services are being provided to address these needs?

    g.   If the youth is intellectually disabled, what services are being provided by the Office of Development Disabilities? Are Independent Living and employment training services making reasonable accommodations for the youth's disabilities?

    h.   Is the youth receiving SSI if eligible?

10.  Is youth's record clear?

    a.   Has credit been checked to ensure that youth was not a victim of identity theft? If youth was a victim of identity theft, has record been cleaned to ensure that youth's poor credit does not impact future educational or housing opportunities?

    b.   If youth had a juvenile record, has record been expunged or sealed?

## Box 2: Checklist for Developing a Transition Plan with Your Youth Client

### Living Arrangements

Where will you live after leaving foster care?

❑   Own apartment/house

❑   Apartment/house with roommate

*Continued*

## Box 2: Checklist for Developing a Transition Plan with Your Youth Client *Continued*

- ❏ College dormitory
- ❏ With parents
- ❏ With relatives
- ❏ With friends of family
- ❏ With former foster parents
- ❏ Long-term medical facility
- ❏ Unsure/don't know
- ❏ Other

### Medical/Health

Do you know the names and dosages of your current medications? Do you know how to get your prescriptions refilled?

Do you know how to contact the public health care provider in your county or parish?

Do you have a Medicaid Waiver?

If not, have you been referred for a Medicaid Waiver?

Do you have a primary care physician to call when you need medical care?

### Independent Living Skills

Have you completed a Life Skills Assessment?

Did you complete an Independent Living Skills Program?

Do you know how to search for resources?

Do you know how to use the Internet to obtain information?

Do you have an e-mail account?

Are you participating in a transition program?

Are you saving money for when you exit foster care?

Do you have a savings/checking account?

### Education

What are your education goals?

What is the highest educational level that you have completed?

Are you currently

- ❏ attending high school
- ❏ pursuing a high school diploma

- ❏ pursuing a GED
- ❏ attending a prevocational program
- ❏ attending college

Have you received information and procedures for

- ❏ applying for college/vocational program
- ❏ applying for scholarships
- ❏ applying for financial aid
- ❏ applying for Educational and Training Voucher Program/all equivalent programs

Have you taken the ACT, SAT, or any other college entrance tests?

## Important Documents

Do you have the following:

- ❏ Birth certificate
- ❏ Social Security card
- ❏ Driver's license or State ID card
- ❏ Insurance cards (auto, medical, other)
- ❏ Medical records
- ❏ Diploma/certificate
- ❏ Resume
- ❏ Life book
- ❏ Letter from state agency noting the dates in foster care and the case identification number
- ❏ List of resources
- ❏ Independent Living Skills Program providers
- ❏ Emergency contacts
- ❏ Relatives' addresses and phone numbers
- ❏ Copy of pertinent court orders

# CHAPTER NINE

## Taking on the System
# The Power of Children's Lawyers and Impact Litigation to Reform the Child Welfare System

By Ira Lustbader

### PART I: MAYA'S STORY

*The Shelter is full of chaos and it hasn't been a refuge at all. I
have missed five months of school. . . . Since being at the Shelter
everything I've ever loved has vanished. My family, my clean record,
all my belongings and most importantly my opportunity to be an
everyday teenager.*

**Maya, age 17, Atlanta, Georgia**
**Letter from Children's Emergency Shelter, DeKalb County, GA,
2001**

The author acknowledges the tremendous support from Linda Pace in Georgia and Anne
Sublett in Oklahoma, two extraordinary children's attorneys who were instrumental in the
preparation of this chapter, and whose tireless efforts made a profound difference in the lives
of the two young women profiled here and so many other children through their work.

Maya, 16 years old, entered the Georgia foster care system in 2001 after a severe beating by her stepfather. According to reports from extended family, the abuse and neglect she suffered began long before then. Maya's father was a drug dealer who abused Maya's mother. Maya's mother had become pregnant with Maya when she was 16 years old, while she lived briefly with Maya's father and his wife. Maya was two years old when her mother left her with relatives in New York and joined the Army. Her mother then married Maya's stepfather, and Maya went to live with them when she was six years old. Maya's mother went on to have three children with Maya's stepfather. The family moved around a lot, and Maya's stepfather drank heavily. Like Maya's biological father, he physically abused her mother, who was in and out of battered women's shelters. After one really bad incident, Maya, then 14 years old, left to stay with family members in New Jersey.

It was then that Maya learned her biological father had been sentenced to three life terms in prison. Maya recalls a single prison visit with her dad, but there was no bond between them. When the living situation with her New Jersey relatives did not work out, Maya moved back in with her mother and stepfather. Shortly after, they all moved to Atlanta, Georgia.

In 2001, someone at Maya's school reported that Maya's stepfather was abusing her. The Georgia child welfare agency removed Maya from her home and immediately placed her in the notorious DeKalb County Children's Emergency Shelter. At least four times over the course of her first 10 months in state custody, Maya ran away from the shelter, was arrested, put in jail, and returned back to the shelter, only to run away again. Before being removed from her home, Maya had been getting all A's and B's in school, and her aptitude scores showed that she was functioning at the 12th grade level. After she was removed from her home, however, Maya attended at least five different high schools in 9th grade alone, and her grades slipped.

The emergency shelter in DeKalb County, like a similar emergency shelter in neighboring Fulton County (the two counties comprise much of metro Atlanta), was a dirty, overcrowded, dangerous warehouse for children ages 11 to 17 in Atlanta. The shelter conditions were shocking by any standard. Children used rows of open cubicles as living and sleeping spaces, with no privacy. Each child was given a small, unlocked trunk to store belongings, which were frequently stolen. Bathrooms were strewn with used sanitary napkins on the floor, and the backed-up toilets were often unusable and filled with waste. Children of all ages and abilities basically read magazines between cigarette breaks in the single-room shelter "school." Shelter staff provided no supervision or programming and spent most of the time hanging out in an office avoiding the children. Some staff would fight the children; others had sex with them. Children went in and out at all hours, walking right into what Maya described as a "bad neighborhood" overrun by drug dealers and gangs. The violence and exploitation just spilled back and forth between the shelter and the surrounding neighborhood. Gang activity, violence, sexual assault, drug use, and prostitution were rampant. The kids even had names for the abandoned buildings where the exploitation took place, such as the White House and the Pentagon. The most predictable presence at the shelter was the police, who showed up whenever things got out of control, and hauled youth to jail for days, weeks, or more, only to discharge them back to the shelter. The state's child welfare system, itself overburdened, mismanaged, and out of control, simply had nowhere to appropriately house the abused and neglected children it was supposed to protect.

Maya herself got caught up in the cycle of arrests at the shelter, which is how she met Linda Pace, a longtime Legal Aid attorney representing kids on delinquency charges. Maya technically had an attorney assigned to her child welfare case as a child in foster care, but, as Maya recalls, she never met that attorney, and never had anyone claiming to represent her at any of her foster care hearings in court. This was not unusual, because at the time only two lawyers in DeKalb County were assigned to represent approximately 1,000 kids in foster care, making effective legal representation impossible.

Pace recalled first meeting Maya when she began representing her in her delinquency cases:

> She was short, cute, animated, easy to talk to, with intelligent eyes and big glasses gracing her round face. I represented Maya on several of her shelter cases. This is what got me going out to the shelter. There was a "revolving door" between detention and the shelter with the shelter staff filing charges on kids so they could get them locked

up and out of the shelter. They were basically using detention as a placement alternative.

Over the next 10 months, Pace helped Maya successfully resolve various criminal charges that arose out of events at the shelter. The state then moved Maya to a "boot camp" for several weeks. What followed was a series of unsuccessful reunification attempts with Maya's mother and stepfather, which always resulted in Maya ending up back in the shelter.

The state then moved Maya into a foster home that lasted one night because, as Maya described, the house was "nasty" and "filthy" and didn't have hot water or food. Again, Maya was brought back to the shelter. This time, though, Maya would soon learn, the plan for her was different. As soon as she arrived, Maya was directed to the shelter administration office with three other teenagers; several police officers guarded the shelter office door to make sure the kids couldn't leave. Maya and the other kids were told to get in a van, or else they would be locked up in jail (a realistic threat since that happened repeatedly). They got in the van and drove for hours with three staff who said they didn't know exactly where they were going. Finally, one of the staff said they were going to a "group home," and showed them a pamphlet that, as Maya recalled, described "a treatment center, behavioral—behavior center, something." But when they finally stopped driving, some 250 miles away in Savannah, the kids realized they were at a large lockdown psychiatric institution. Maya remembered that moment:

So I ran. We all ran, all four kids ran. We didn't know where we were running to, but we were running, got maybe four blocks away. Then paddy wagons and police were all over the place.

Maya was unnecessarily institutionalized for weeks. No one could tell her why she was there. One staff member said to her, "There has to be a reason why you're here." Maya remembered her response: "I said, 'Sir, there's nothing wrong with me.'" Maya was forced to take various pills, supposedly for sleeping or depression. "I never saw daylight … because I didn't have points." (Children had to earn points with good behavior for the most basic privileges, such as going outside.) Maya was initially denied access to her lawyer, but she was eventually able to contact Pace, who arranged to bring Maya back to DeKalb County. The judge was none too pleased with Maya's treatment, and he ordered her released back to her mother's custody. Her mother then consented to allow Maya, then age 17, to move to New Jersey to live with relatives.

Even though Maya finally got out of state custody and found some stability, she thought often about how her experience in the foster care system had hurt her and so many kids like her. In 2002, shortly after she was arrested at the shelter and Pace was assigned as her attorney, Maya became one of seven named plaintiff children in a federal class action lawsuit on behalf of a class of all 3,000 children in metropolitan Atlanta in the state's foster care system, which became known as the *Kenny A.* case. Defendants included the Georgia governor and state officials responsible for the child welfare system. The plaintiffs' legal team included lawyers at Children's Rights, a national nonprofit advocacy group that specializes in bringing impact litigation on behalf of abused and neglected kids; and lawyers at Bondurant, Mixson & Elmore, LLP, a law firm in Atlanta with a proud history of taking on civil rights cases. Maya and the other plaintiff children brought the litigation through their adult "Next Friends." Pace, who was Maya's trusted lawyer on shelter-related criminal charges, and who had a deep understanding of how systemic failures gravely harmed Maya and children like her, readily agreed to serve as Maya's Next Friend.

The *Kenny A.* lawsuit alleged that long-ignored systemic failings harmed foster children and placed them all at an unreasonable risk of harm. The system's grave failings, many of which Maya experienced firsthand, included, among other things, a gross shortage of safe, appropriate homes for children; children warehoused in unsuitable emergency shelters and other facilities; children regularly bounced many times from one inappropriate home or facility to another, and often far from their home communities; inadequate monitoring and oversight of homes and facilities for foster care children; and children maltreated while in foster care custody. The lawsuit asserted that the defendants violated children's federal and state constitutional rights, most notably the right to be reasonably free from harm while in state custody under the substantive due process clause of the Fourteenth Amendment, as well as provisions of federal and state statutes that governed the safety

**127**

and well-being of children in state custody. The plaintiff children in *Kenny A.* sought only injunctive relief to fix the system (not money damages).

In 2002, the *Kenny A.* plaintiffs sought a preliminary injunction to stop admissions to the shelter and to shut it down because the horrible conditions there were hurting so many children. The federal court held an evidentiary hearing over five days, and Maya gave detailed firsthand testimony of what she went through at the DeKalb shelter. Plaintiffs also called the highly respected juvenile court Judge Robin Nash to testify about children being cycled in and out of the shelter, including Maya. (Judge Nash was the judge who finally released Maya from custody.) Maya's final words to the court, as her Next Friend Pace looked on, were, "I'd like everyone to know that the shelter isn't a good place for any kid to live. It's not good at all."

Maya's brave testimony was critical to the success that followed. Toward the end of the hearing, the state child welfare agency commissioner promised that both shelters would be closed within a few months. The federal judge, who found that "few concrete steps were taken to close the shelters before this lawsuit was filed," took the commissioner at his word. Consequently, the federal court denied an injunction to close the shelters "without prejudice," inviting the plaintiffs to come back if the shelters weren't closed as promised. That was not necessary. Both shelters were closed within months, and at least one dark chapter in the system was over.

But there was so much more to do. The shelters were one symptom of a completely broken child welfare agency. Over the next three years of intensive litigation, millions of pages of documents were produced and analyzed, file reviews of hundreds of children were conducted, more than 70 depositions were taken, and numerous expert reports were filed. Then just before trial, the parties began negotiating a comprehensive court-enforceable reform plan (known as a "consent decree").

After six months of negotiations under the direction of a court-appointed mediator, the federal court approved a comprehensive settlement between the plaintiff children and state officials in October 2005. The consent decree sets enforceable standards for the agency's infrastructure, accountability, and resources and established required performance outcomes on 31 key issues. Among its many requirements, the consent decree sharply curtailed the use of any emergency or temporary housing and other group facilities and heightened licensing and monitoring requirements for all homes and facilities that house children in foster care. In 2006, the federal court also approved "right to counsel" consent decrees between the plaintiff children and county officials in Fulton and DeKalb Counties, guaranteeing every child in foster care the right to counsel, and effective legal representation, throughout their entire involvement with the juvenile court. Today, eight years after the settlements, major improvements have taken hold, but some big problems remain, and the lawsuit continues. Among the improvements, emergency shelters are no longer used, oversight of facilities and homes has increased, and parent-child visitation for kids with a goal of reunification has improved. On the right to counsel, staffing and support has vastly improved, with caseloads for lawyers dropping from more than 500 children per lawyer to well under 100 children per lawyer. Improvements in caseloads, support and quality of legal representation were so significant that the "right to counsel" settlements have successfully closed. The full case history can be found at http://www.childrensrights.org/reform-campaigns /legal-cases/georgia/.

## PART II: GINA'S STORY

In 2003, Gina, then nine years old, entered Oklahoma's foster care system after telling school staff that her stepfather was sexually abusing her. Gina and her six siblings were taken into state custody. Gina later disclosed that her stepfather's friends had raped her as well, and that her stepfather repeatedly beat her and her siblings with a hanger and a water hose. Gina had been afraid to tell anyone because her stepfather said he would throw her out of the house if she told.

Before the day when Gina disclosed the abuse she suffered to her teachers, the Oklahoma child protection agency had received 16 reports of suspected child abuse concerning Gina, the first when she was six weeks old. The list of allegations—some completely ignored, some substantiated, some ruled out—included multiple counts of physical and sexual abuse, medical neglect, malnutrition, and substance abuse in the home. Yet for nine years the state failed to intervene and protect Gina.

When the state finally did intervene, the failures in Oklahoma's foster care system re-victimized Gina. From 2003 to 2008, Gina was bounced around 18 times among homes and facilities, where she was the repeated victim of physical, sexual, and emotional abuse. During that time, Gina's case was assigned to 55 different caseworkers and 44 different supervisors.

Gina's first placement was a month in the notoriously overcrowded, poorly supervised emergency shelter in Tulsa. That was followed by a two-week stint in a foster home that the state agency had already deemed unsuitable. Next came a year in a "kinship" home from which Gina was eventually removed due to child abuse allegations. The state then bounced Gina back and forth over the next six months between a foster home and an emergency shelter in another county.

The state then moved Gina, 11 years old, back home for a poorly supervised trial reunification with her mother. Gina had never received the intensive mental health treatment she needed to address the abuse by her stepfather. Two of Gina's brothers, who were living with her mother when she moved back home, looked just like her stepfather, which immediately triggered flashbacks of her stepfather's abuse. Gina decompensated and was removed from her mother's home and put in a psychiatric hospital for a month.

When Gina was discharged from the hospital, the state then placed her directly into yet another emergency shelter for a week. This was followed by more than a year in a supposedly specialized "therapeutic foster home" where Gina was sexually exploited by several other children in the home. While there, Gina was sent on weekend visits with relatives who were purportedly interested in adopting her, although she felt unsafe with them. That home was so filthy that a caseworker reported she was nearly overwhelmed by the smell just standing at the front door.

At this point, Gina, almost 13, again experienced flashbacks of her stepfather's abuse. After telling a teacher about her self-inflicted wounds and thoughts of suicide, Gina was hospitalized again, for more than a month, where the treatment focus was post-traumatic stress disorder (PTSD). Gina reported that another patient in the facility sexually molested her, but it was never investigated. When she was discharged from the hospital, the state put her back into the prior therapeutic foster home that had inadequately cared for her. She stayed there for four months. Over the next several months, Gina was moved among several unsuitable foster homes, including a trial adoptive placement with a foster father who had been previously accused of sexual abuse. The instability and continued lack of intensive consistent mental health care were too much to overcome. Gina began cutting herself again and engaging in other self-harming behaviors.

Around this time, in 2007, Anne Sublett, a partner at Conner & Winters LLP, a prestigious Tulsa-based law firm, was appointed to represent Gina. Sublett began providing pro bono representation to children in abuse and neglect cases in 1994, when her firm volunteered to take cases in which the public defender's office had a conflict of interest (usually as a result of representing the parents in a related criminal case). In 2000, Sublett's county bar association began a program to recruit and train lawyers throughout the Tulsa community to represent kids. With Sublett in a leadership role, Tulsa Lawyers for Children, a non-profit organization that works with lawyers and law students throughout Tulsa, has since given voice to nearly 4,000 children since its formation.

Sublett recently looked back on first meeting Gina:

She was a deeply troubled young woman entering her teen years with poor skills for negotiating what is a challenging time of life for kids with none of her baggage. Gina was desperate to please people and to gain the attention of others—of anyone, in fact. In Oklahoma, a child's lawyer in an abuse case is required to represent the child's expressed interest rather than her best interest. Getting past Gina's intense desire to please others and to attract attention in order to discern what she actually wanted was always a challenge. For example, after several conversations with Gina about her mother, their relationship and her mother's plans to marry yet another boyfriend and move to Florida, I filed a motion to terminate the mother's parental rights. As I prepared for the trial, however, it became clear that Gina's mother's attorney intended to call Gina as a witness. As I worked with Gina to prepare her for the trial, it became clear that it was highly unlikely that Gina would risk her mother's disapproval by testifying that she wanted parental rights terminated. We called off the trial and went back to the drawing board.

After Gina was abruptly pulled from a preadoptive home because of prior sexual abuse allegations against the foster father, the state placed her back in the Tulsa emergency shelter for three days. That was followed by a move to another foster home for six weeks. Confused, angry, and deeply traumatized, Gina thought she wanted to go back to the trial adoptive family, as she had no idea why she had been suddenly taken out of that home. She also thought things could work out with her mother. Meanwhile, her desperate need for counseling remained unmet, and after only two weeks with her new foster family, she began cutting herself again. In early 2008, Gina, at 14, was admitted to a psychiatric hospital for the third time in five years.

Sublett and Gina eventually developed enough of a relationship to identify a safe way, one that Gina genuinely wanted, to end the cycle of constant moves and unimaginable trauma the Oklahoma foster care system was inflicting on her. Sublett recalled the plan they put together:

> What I was ultimately able to discern through our meetings and conversations, and to facilitate, was that Gina wanted to be with her younger brothers ... who had been adopted by her aunt. Despite what [the state agency] had been saying and apparently believed, Gina's aunt wanted her as well. So, rather than terminate Gina's mother's parental rights, we were able to place Gina in a permanent guardianship with her aunt.

Through her trusting relationship with an attorney who sought to achieve her goals, Gina was finally able to find a safe, permanent home, ending her time in state custody.

Looking back, with more than 18 years of providing pro bono representation for abused and neglected children in state custody, Sublett has witnessed the harmful impact on so many kids flowing from long-ignored failures in the Oklahoma foster care system:

> [C]hildren taken out of abusive homes were placed in foster homes and institutions where they suffered additional abuse and neglect. I have visited foster homes in which I would not leave my dog, much less a child. Case workers, often with inadequate training, had such

**132**

high caseloads that it was simply impossible for them to see regularly all of the children to whom they were assigned and to know the kids well enough to learn their stories. Turnover among workers was so high and children's placement changes so frequent that all too often the only constant adult in a child's life was the child's lawyer. I became convinced that the profound change needed for ... our foster care system would only come through statewide, large-scale litigation.

Seeing that agency-wide improvements in the system could help Gina and many children like her, Sublett agreed to serve as Gina's adult Next Friend when Gina became a named plaintiff, before she left state custody, in a 2008 federal class action lawsuit filed on behalf of all 10,000 children in the Oklahoma foster care system. The lawsuit, known as *D.G. v. Henry*, alleged that long-known and ignored failures in Oklahoma's foster care system harmed children and subjected them to risks of harm in violation of their federal constitutional rights. Many of the system's deficiencies—including grossly poor and untimely investigations of reports of child abuse, frequent maltreatment of children in foster care, excessively high child welfare worker caseloads, an extreme lack of appropriate foster homes, and high placement instability—had played a role in the almost incomprehensible trauma Gina suffered while in state custody. As with the *Kenny A.* case in Georgia, the core claim in the *D.G. v. Henry* lawsuit asserted that state officials violated children's substantive due process rights to be reasonably free from harm while in state custody.

The legal team for plaintiffs in *D.G. v. Henry* included lawyers from the national advocacy group Children's Rights and lawyers from several prominent Oklahoma firms, including Frederick Dorwart Lawyers LLP; Seymour & Graham LLP; Day, Edwards & Christensen LLP; and the international law firm of Kaye Scholar LLP. Like Pace, who was Maya's Next Friend in the *Kenny A.* litigation in Georgia, Sublett recognized that impact litigation could "lift the veil off our state's dirty little secret: its own abuse and neglect of children in its care" and spur needed systemic reform.

As in the Georgia litigation, fact-finding in the *D.G. v. Henry* case included production and review of millions of pages of documents, more than 70 depositions, file reviews of hundreds of children's case files, and numerous expert reports. Gina's case was highlighted in a scathing expert report showing the Oklahoma system's numerous extreme departures from widely recognized standards of social work practice. The litigation exposed shocking failures in the Oklahoma foster care system, and in particular a near total lack of accountability by the state board of commissioners that was charged with overseeing the child welfare agency.

After more than three years of hard-fought litigation and the federal court's denial of motions to throw the case out without a trial, the parties reached an extraordinary settlement agreement that was approved by the federal court in May 2012. The settlement gives broad authority to three "Co-Neutrals" to set improvement standards in 15 different areas of historically poor performance. They can approve or disapprove of the child welfare agency's strategies for meeting those standards, determine whether those standards have been met, and require the agency to undertake additional remedies if the state fails to make sufficient progress. Importantly, the Co-Neutrals' decisions can be converted into enforceable court orders. The full case history can be found at http://www.childrensrights.org /reform-campaigns/legal-cases/oklahoma/.

While implementation is still in its early stages, the current plan under the settlement calls for improvements in the screening, investigation, and reporting of abuse and neglect for children in foster care; reducing the use of shelter care for older children and eliminating it entirely for younger children; and bringing the workloads of all case workers down to manageable levels. The long-serving head of the child welfare agency has resigned. The state abolished the board of commissioners, which, as the lawsuit proved, had completely failed to oversee the agency and the care and protection of children who depended on it. Now, agency oversight will rest with the governor.

## PART III: ACCOUNTABILITY AND BETTER OUTCOMES FOR KIDS: IMPACT LITIGATION TO REFORM THE HIDDEN REVICTIMIZATION OF CHILDREN IN STATE FOSTER CARE SYSTEMS

The stories recounted in this chapter from Georgia and Oklahoma highlight the harrowing experiences of Maya and Gina while in state foster care custody. One cannot help but be humbled by the strength of these young women. These stories also are about Pace and Sublett, extraordinary lawyers providing direct legal representation for vulnerable children, one a seasoned public interest lawyer, the other a partner in a private firm with a pro bono children's practice. Not only did Pace and Sublett make a difference at critical points in the lives of Maya and Gina, these two lawyers helped to change the systems in their states by playing a key role in impact litigation. (See Box 1, "The Role of Next Friends in Children's Rights Litigation.")

Under the right circumstances, child welfare impact litigation is a powerful tool to ensure that abused and neglected children receive the protection and services they deserve and are entitled to under the law. Complementing the essential work of attorneys providing direct representation to individual children in juvenile and family courts, impact litigation approaches problems in the aggregate. To borrow a powerful metaphor some have used, picture a foster care system as a large house. If the foundation and infrastructure are defective, and there are broken windows and glass and other dangers throughout the house, some kids in the house are getting hurt every day, and *all of them* are at risk of getting hurt every day. Impact litigation seeks to fix the house.

The basic charge of every state's child welfare system is uncontroversial: keep children safe and preserve families whenever possible, and when intervention is necessary, provide for children's ongoing safety, well-being, and permanency needs. When government intervention is truly necessary and children must be removed, government custody is a temporary solution. Children must be kept safe and given the placements, services, and treatment to address all their needs. This includes closely monitoring children and the places they are housed, utilizing the least restrictive and most family-like housing matched to meet children's individual needs, ensuring appropriate education and special education services, sibling and family connections, community connections, health care, and services to prepare older youth for a successful transition when they leave the system as young adults. Permanency means a loving, permanent home, outside of state custody, with family or kin whenever possible, or through adoption or guardianship when family or kin placements are not achievable.

The size and scope of the nation's child welfare systems are considerable. The most recent data, from 2011, shows approximately 3.4 million reports of abuse or neglect, covering more than 6 million children.[1] Reports of abuse or neglect involving approximately 680,000 children were "substantiated" (i.e., abuse or neglect was concluded to have occurred).[2] Roughly 400,000 children were in state foster care systems on any given day.[3] About 26,000 children "aged out" (were emancipated) from the foster care system.[4] In 2010, approximately $29 billion in federal, state, and local funds were expended for child welfare programs.[5] Importantly, children of color and children living in poverty are disproportionately represented in these systems.[6]

Unfortunately, children are often revictimized by the very systems that exist to protect them. Major systemic failings, such as those highlighted in the stories of Maya and Gina, can include

- a drastic shortage of foster homes;
- excessive caseloads/workloads of frontline case managers and supervisors;
- inadequate training of child welfare staff;
- inadequate assessments and planning for children;

---

1. U.S. DEP'T OF HEALTH & HUM. SERV., CHILD. BUREAU, CHILD MALTREATMENT 2011, at 5-6 (2012), *available at* http://www.acf.hhs.gov/programs/cb/resource/child-maltreatment-2011.
2. *Id.* at xi.
3. *See* U.S. DEP'T OF HEALTH & HUM. SERV., CHILD. BUREAU, THE AFCARS REPORT, PRELIMINARY FY 2011 ESTIMATES AS OF JULY 2012 at 1 (2012), *available at* http://www.acf .hhs.gov/sites/default/files/cb/afcarsreport19.pdf.
4. *See id.* at 3.
5. *See Total Child Welfare Expenditures in SFY 2010, All Sources*, STATE CHILD WELFARE POLICY DATABASE (last visited Aug. 6, 2013), http://www.childwelfarepolicy.org/maps /single?id=264.
6. *See, e.g.*, ROBERT B. HILL, CASEY-CSSP ALLIANCE FOR RACIAL EQUITY IN CHILD WELFARE, AN ANALYSIS OF RACIAL/ETHNIC DISPROPORTIONALITY AND DISPARITY AT THE NATIONAL, STATE, AND COUNTY LEVELS, *available at* http://www.aecf.org/~/media/Pubs/Topics /Child%20Welfare%20Permanence/Other/AnAnalysisofRacialEthnicDisproportionalityand /Bob%20Hill%20report%20natl%20state%20racial%20disparity%202007.pdf; *see also* Sandra Stukes Chipungu & Tricia B. Bent-Goodley, *Meeting the Challenges of Contemporary Foster Care*, 14 THE FUTURE OF CHILDREN 75 (2004), *available at* http://www.princeton .edu/futureofchildren/publications/journals/article/index.xml?journalid=40&articleid=135 &sectionid=887.

- inadequate training and supports for foster parents;
- inadequate safety monitoring, worker-child visitation, and licensing practices;
- inadequate supervision of private providers that provide housing and services;
- inadequate medical, dental, and mental health services;
- inadequate permanency services (reunification, adoption, guardianship);
- inadequate services to enable older youth to transition to adulthood; and
- inadequate management information systems to track individual children and aggregate data to ensure informed decision making.

These systemic problems, all too often, result in specific harms (re-victimization) and risks of such harms to children, including

- maltreatment of children in foster care;
- separation of children from siblings and interference with sibling and other family relationships, and loss of community;
- misuse and overuse of shelters and other facilities and institutions for children;
- multiple moves among numerous homes and facilities;
- inadequately treated and deteriorating health issues; and
- denial of opportunities for permanent homes and excessive stays in state custody.

And yet, aside from the occasional child death covered by the news media, very often long-standing and deep-rooted failures in these systems, and the revictimization they cause, remain hidden from public view. Why? For one thing, state confidentiality laws shroud a lot of the operations of state child welfare systems in secrecy. Additionally, children in foster care do not vote and do not have a powerful lobby, especially at the state level. Finally, there is little to no federal or state accountability when these systems fail.

In the right circumstances, with the strength of powerful advocacy partnerships, child welfare impact litigation seeks to bring accountability and improvements to children's lives. The lawsuits are brought as class actions, governed by Federal Rule of Civil Procedure 23. While conditions vary from state to state, legal claims in impact lawsuits aimed at systemic reform have included the following:

- substantive and procedural violations of the Due Process Clause of the Fourteenth Amendment to the United States Constitution;
- violations of liberty, privacy, and associational rights under the First, Ninth, and Fourteenth Amendments to the United States Constitution;
- violations of the Equal Protection Clause of the Fourteenth Amendment to the United States Constitution;
- violations of federal statutory rights under
  - the Adoption Assistance and Child Welfare Act of 1980, as amended by the Adoption and Safe Families Act of 1997 (the "Adoption Assistance Act");
  - the Multiethnic Placement Act of 1994, as amended by the Inter-ethnic Adoption Provisions of 1996;
  - the Early and Periodic Screening, Diagnosis, and Treatment (EPSDT) Program of the Medicaid Act;
  - the Individuals with Disabilities Education Improvement Act (IDEIA), still commonly referred to as the Individuals with Disabilities Education Act or IDEA;
  - the Americans with Disabilities Act (ADA); and
  - Title VI of the Civil Rights Act.
- breach of the federal-state contract under Title IV-E of the Social Security Act;
- violations of state statutory rights or state judicially created rights; and
- violations of state constitutional rights.

The goals of child welfare impact litigation are to shine a light and bring accountability to government systems, to vindicate and strengthen the legal rights of children, and, most of all, to bring measurable improvements to children's lives. That includes, for example, shutting down the dangerous emergency shelters in Atlanta and overhauling the system to monitor safety and performance in Oklahoma, alongside numerous other measurable positive outcomes. Among other improvements, impact litigation has produced major programmatic shifts away from unnecessary, harmful, and expensive institutional care, in favor of supported family-based care, as has occurred in Tennessee and Connecticut.

Reforms won by Children's Rights, where I have worked since 1999, vary with each jurisdiction and consent decrees are often modified by agreement of the parties over time. They cover a wide range of issues, with infrastructure and process requirements, along with outcome measures, all designed to fix systemic failures and improve children's lives. Areas of remediation have included reporting and investigating abuse and neglect; staff qualifications, training, caseloads, and supervision; placement and supervision of children; safety monitoring, visitation, and licensing of homes and facilities; reunification and adoption services; medical, dental, and mental health care; foster parent recruitment, retention, and approval; statewide information systems; quality assurance systems; supervision of private provider agencies; and guaranteeing children the right to adequate and effective counsel. Importantly, impact litigation also creates the space for national and local expert technical assistance, collaboration among advocates and state officials, creative solutions, and the application of best practices in the field. (See Box 2, "Resources on Federal Claims, Class Certification, and Consent Decrees in Child Welfare Litigation.") And perhaps most importantly, these reform efforts have achieved dramatic and measureable improvements in safety, permanency and well-being for kids.

To be sure, child welfare impact litigation presents serious legal and factual challenges, and consumes considerable time and resources. Cases are often defended and litigated vigorously for years, either to the eve of trial or through trial. While consent decrees are a powerful tool for positive change, progress and improvements can be uneven and certainly never come fast enough. The country's years-long economic downturn has decimated many state budgets and safety nets for vunerable children and families. This feeds into a misguided perception that we have no other choice but to tolerate dangerous resource-starved systems for abused and neglected kids. Similarly, there's often an undercurrent (if not an overtly attempted legal defense) in this field that the shared normative failure of many state child welfare systems somehow insulates a particular state from the legal (let alone moral and human rights–related) imperative to operate a system at a basic level of protection and dignity for children.

**139**

These challenges are real, but they cannot outweigh the reality of children such as Maya and Gina being re-victimized by the government systems that exist to protect them. When child welfare systems fail at their most basic charges, and state officials lack the will or ability to remedy the problems, impact litigation remains a critical force for social change. I have had the privilege to work on children's rights reform campaigns in many states around the country, and to work alongside people like Pace and Sublett. These children's lawyers not only fought for and changed the lives of individual children, they also helped take on the system.

## Box 1: The Role of Next Friends in Children's Rights Litigation

As minors, Maya and Gina could bring their cases only through an adult "Next Friend," who are identified by name in the lawsuit, whereas plaintiff children are identified by pseudonyms only. The role of Next Friends in federal cases is governed by Fed. R. Civ. P. 17(c). Essentially, the law requires a Next Friend to be dedicated to pursuing the litigation on behalf of the child for as long as it takes, and not have any conflicts that would prevent him or her from serving in this important role. While a relationship between the child and Next Friend is surely desirable, the law allows Next Friends in some circumstances to be strangers to the children they represent, given the reality that children in state custody often move around and lack stable adult relationships in their lives. Given their knowledge of the system, Next Friends like Pace and Sublett have provided—and continue to provide—valuable strategic insight to plaintiffs' counsel throughout the litigation.

## Box 2: Resources on Federal Claims, Class Certification, and Consent Decrees in Child Welfare Litigation

On challenges to plaintiffs' constitutional and statutory claims, see the decisions in the Georgia *Kenny A.* case on motions to dismiss[7] and summary judgment.[8] On class certification, see the appellate decision in the Oklahoma *D.G. v. Henry* case;[9] but following the Supreme Court's decision in *Wal-Mart v. Dukes*,[10] see also *M.D. v. Perry*,[11] in which the Fifth Circuit Court of Appeals vacated and remanded a class certification because the district court failed to apply "rigorous analysis" under *Wal-Mart*, and the district court on remand upheld class certification.[12] Consent decrees in all of Children's Rights cases can be found at http://www.childrensrights .org. Additionally, the federal Children's Bureau, part of the Administration for Children and Families (ACF) of the Department of Health and Human Services (HHS), maintains a useful resource for learning about child welfare litigation at https://www.childwelfare.gov/management/ reform/litigation.cfm. Finally, the Children's Rights Litigation Committee of the Section on Litigation of the American Bar Association maintains a comprehensive Web resource on children's right to counsel at www.ambar .org/FosteringJustice

---

7.  218 F.R.D. 277 (N.D. Ga. 2003).

8.  356 F. Supp. 2d 1353 (N.D. Ga. 2005).

9.  594 F.3d 1188 (10th Circ. 2010) (affirming class certification).

10.  Wal-Mart Stores, Inc. v. Dukes, 131 S. Ct. 2541 (2011).

11.  675 F.3d 832 (5th Cir. 2012).

12.  No. 2:11–CV–84, 2013 WL 4537955, at *1 (S.D. Tex. Aug. 27, 2013). *See also* Connor B. v. Patrick, in which a Massachusetts district court denied a motion to decertify a class following Wal-Mart, 278 F.R.D. 30 (D.Mass.), but then dismissed the case under Fed. R. Civ. P. 52. Connor B. *ex rel* Vigurs, Civil Action No. 10-30073-WGY, 2013 WL 6181454 (D. Mass. Nov. 22, 2013). That ruling is currently on appeal.

# INDEX